AVERAGE
70KG
D**KHEAD

MOTIVATIONAL LESSONS FROM AN
EX-ARMY SPECIAL FORCES DOCTOR

DAN PRONK

**To find out more about this book or
to contact the author, please visit:
www.vividpublishing.com.au/70kg**

Copyright © 2019 Dan Pronk

ISBN: 978-1-925846-74-4
Published by Vivid Publishing
A division of Fontaine Publishing Group
P.O. Box 948, Fremantle
Western Australia 6959
www.vividpublishing.com.au

 A catalogue record for this
book is available from the
National Library of Australia

CONTENTS

Introduction

The first point that I would like to make before we get started relates to the very ethos of this book, and that is this book is imperfect. As you read you will no doubt find typos, spelling and grammatical errors for which, while they are certainly not intentional, I make no apologies. For the American audience, the book has been written using English spelling protocols, so there aren't as many spelling mistakes as you might think you're picking up! One of the key principles I want to convey in this book is to take action and get started, and the process of meticulously revising and refining this manuscript would have been the antithesis of that principle. This book serves as an elaboration of some of my Instagram posts that seemed to capture the imagination of some and through their comments and messages I was humbled to learn that I had helped to motivate and inspire them to keep moving forward in life. I truly hope that at least one of the topics discussed herein resonates with you and inspires you to take a current endeavor to the next level or overcome the mental barriers to start something new. We only get one crack at this life, so make it count! Let's get started.

Average 70kg Dickhead

The term *average 70kg dickhead* stems from a conversation that I had in my early twenties with my flat mate at the time. We were both keen triathletes and had just returned from a training session at the gym where there had been a humungous rock-ape type bloke lifting ridiculous weights and screaming for the whole world to hear as he did so. The subsequent discussion that my friend and I were having centred around whether being able to lift that amount of weight in the gym necessarily translated into any practical application, specifically fighting. I put this query to my friend and he had replied with "surely if he can lift those weights in the gym he could pick up and throw your average 70kg dickhead". The term resonated with me as it is precisely as I have always, and continue to, see myself – an average 70kg dickhead.

I confess that many of the experiences that I have had over my life have been far from average, and some of the things that I may have accomplished in my professional career have been slightly right of centre on the bell curve.

That said, when it boils down to me specifically I am average, weigh roughly 70kg, and as my wife loves to remind me, am indeed very capable of being a bit of a dickhead. I was born into an average middle-class Australian family to an army dad and a speech therapist mum. I have one brother and we had a cat growing up. Average. I was average throughout my schooling and owing to my dad's army postings went to 8 different schools, getting expelled from one. I eventually got through grade 12 with Cs in physics and math, and grades good enough to get me into university to do something but nowhere near good enough to apply for medical school at the time. I was average at sport for most of my youth, swimming and playing cricket at a regional level in my primary school years. In my later years of high school I took a keen interest in middle-distance running and this was the first time I really devoted myself towards setting goals, and I found myself popping my head up above average by ranking in the top 10 in my State for 1500m in my senior year. Aside from that I had an average amount of friends at school but was never the cool kid. I had girlfriends, but never the hottest girls in the school.

Overall I had a very average upbringing. Don't get me wrong, I certainly wasn't below average or disadvantaged in my upbringing, mine is not an inspirational story of over-coming overwhelming adversity or rising up against huge odds. My family unit was stable, we weren't rich but we had more than enough to get by. I always had a roof over my head, and I never went hungry, quite the opposite – until

ing I was a slightly fat kid. What I'm getting
. the physical and mental tools that were at
...sposal at the beginning of my life were the exact same
set that the majority of society gets allocated, nothing more,
nothing less.

In the 25 years since I left school with average grades
I have managed to become a doctor, join the Australian
Army and pass Special Forces selection, get decorated for
my conduct in action on Special Operations in Afghanistan,
complete specialist medical training, represent Australian
Special Forces medical on an international level, complete
an MBA, co-own a business with multi-million dollar
revenues, buy a Lamborghini and a Ferrari, found an
ambitious startup company building a prototype sports
car with a view to limited production, and get an executive
job running a state-wide medical capability. I've fallen in
a bit of a post-traumatic heap after my time with the army
and managed not only to climb back out of my rut, but to
somehow become a better person because of it. Along the
way I married a fantastic woman and we had three awesome
kids.

I'm as surprised as anyone about some of the events in
my life over the past 25 years, and on reflection I can see
that there's a healthy mix of nature, nurture, amazing role
models, and more than a fair share of lady luck and good
timing to my story. This book is a series of ramblings re-
gurgitated from my mind in an attempt to explain how an
average 70kg dickhead somehow managed to occasionally

squirm his way to above average results. It is not designed to be a memoir of any kind, and follows no particular order, it is simply a series of chapters relating to motivational factors in my life to date and lessons learned along the way.

It is Not the Critic Who Counts

Many readers will recognise the title of this chapter as the opening words from the legendary speech widely known as *The Man in the Arena* delivered by Theodore Roosevelt to a large audience in Paris in the year 1910. If you're unaware of this speech you should look it up, in my opinion it is the most inspirational passage that has ever been uttered and it has fueled my motivation towards many goals in my life.

Failure to see the truth behind this opening line: *It is not the critic that counts* is at the core of why many of us in this life never hit our goals, and why some of us never even set goals in the first instance. It is human nature to be influenced by what others think of us, especially those close to us, and sadly it is also human nature for a lot of people to want to drag down the tall poppies among us. I guess this tendency stems from an inherent insecurity that many have that is worsened by watching others rise above the level of performance that they are at. These people don't have the aptitude or drive to strive towards a goal themselves, so to retain their own sense of self-worth it is crucial for them to do their best to dissuade others from pursuing self-improvement that would lead them to betterment. That way everyone stays at their shitty level and they can feel equal, and not inferior. The way that these people achieve this objective is through criticism of your goals and aspirations. Let me provide an example.

In late 2001 I had been introduced to the world of Army Special Forces through my best mate, who had joined the Australian Special Air Service Regiment (SASR) and was getting ready to deploy to Afghanistan on one of the early rotations of Australia's involvement in the conflict. I had visited him for a holiday to catch up before he deployed and during the trip I had the chance to meet a few of his fellow operators and tour the base they worked out of. I was hooked. A lightbulb flicked on in my mind and I knew instantly that was the career for me. I was already on a trajectory toward being an army doctor, but I decided that from that day forth I would dedicate my very existence toward becoming an army Special Forces doctor. It was a perfect fit in my mind, a way to blend medicine with a physically demanding role, as well as a healthy dose of professional satisfaction and excitement on the side. I dedicated the next six years of my life towards bettering myself with the objective of completing the grueling SASR selection course. I completed my medical schooling, all the while pack marching hundreds of kilometers month-in, month-out, I studied languages, I scuba dived, I rock climbed, I shot handguns and rifles, anything to improve myself in areas that I felt might improve my chances of being suitable for Special Forces service. All the while I stayed quiet about my aspirations, and aside from a few key people in my life who I knew would support me, I didn't tell a soul. Fast forward to 2007 and I had graduated from medical school, completed my compulsory medical internship and a further year of civilian hospital experience, and I was a few months into my posting to my first army unit. Despite having technically been in the army for six years by that stage, all of that time had been spent in civilian schooling and hospitals, so in effect I was only several months into proper military service. That first year "in uniform" was spent doing a series of basic induction courses to learn how to behave as an army officer, as well as apply my medical skill set in the army environment. For all intents and purposes I was a newbie, wet behind the ears. That was the context within which I attended my interview with my army career advisor that year. Now before we go on, I feel it's important to see this interaction from his perspective. From his side of the table he would have seen me as a brand-new baby army doctor who was 30 seconds into his job and was yet to even complete the courses required to become employable in a full capacity in the role, let alone deployable. He didn't know me from a bar of soap, and certainly would have had no idea that I had spent the previous six years sharpening myself physically and mentally for Special Forces selection. Back to my side of the table. As I entered that interview my initial impression of my career advisor was unimpressive. He was overweight, slumped in his chair, wearing his dress uniform poorly, and didn't rise from his seat to greet me when I entered. He was however the person who could have a significant impact on my career, so I looked past my initial impression and pressed on with the start of the interview, trying to put my best foot forward. When asked what my intentions were for my career, I confidently informed him of my plan to do SASR selection and pursue a career with Special Forces. He had been eating his lunch while completing my interview and it was at this point, with a mouth full of food, that he looked up at me in amused disbelief as to what he was hearing and began to draw a deep breath to laugh in my face. In doing so he deeply inhaled a food particle from his mouth which sent him into an explosive coughing fit that caused him to turn red, and then purple, before finally clearing his airways enough to allow him to laugh directly to my face. He proceeded to crap all over my aspirations and let me know that I was sacrificing my opportunity to build a real career by chasing a pipe dream. I had never felt so humiliated in my life; I felt my face redden and my blood pressure rise. The blood vessels in my temples started to throb and I actually felt tears well in my eyes, it was a horrible experience. As you can imagine, the remainder of that interview was icy and unproductive. We ticked the remaining boxes to complete the process and I left the room feeling very angry and very, very small. After taking a few hours to calm down from the humiliation of the interview I decided that showing was better than telling and I strengthened my already robust resolve to pass SASR selection and live my dream of joining Special Forces. I took the negative energy from the interaction with that career advisor and used it to fuel my training from that day on, reliving that experience in my mind during my darker times of physical pain and exhaustion during training. I turned his condescension into rocket fuel for my motivation, if nothing else than to stick my success as far up his arse as possible. I'm not entirely sure how healthy using spite as motivation is, but at that stage it seemed to serve me well. I have subsequently seen spite referred to as a motivator in a couple of books, most notably in "How to be f*cking awesome" by Dan Meredith, which is a refreshing take on the motivational book theme and well worth a read in my opinion.

Had my drive towards the goal of Special Forces selection not have been so well established at the time of my interaction with the career advisor, I imagine that interview may have had a profoundly negative impact on my aspirations, maybe even to the point where I let go of my dreams just because that guy was so sure they were unachievable. Once again, back to that scenario from his perspective, all he would have seen was yet another punk sitting across from him, telling him they were going to be Special Forces. I'm sure he had heard it a hundred times before and that the vast majority of those people never even stepped up for selection, let alone successfully completed the course and joined Special Forces. You see, in my experience, there was no shortage of military members who would have, could have, or were going to do Special Forces selection, except for some small issue that stopped them. I'm sure the army is still full of these people now. Whether they truly believed it themselves or not, there is always a family commitment, a niggling injury, a moral dilemma, the list goes on. Maybe for some of them the reason is legitimate, and they have assessed that the juice of attempting Special Forces selection is not worth the squeeze. They may not be able to commit to the hectic lifestyle of Special Forces due to an unwell family member, a child with special needs or the like. These are legitimate reasons to not make a somewhat selfish career choice, and the people who make them are to be admired. For the most part however, I suspect that no such legitimate reason exists, and these people hide behind these excuses to be able to externalise the reason behind what is actually their own inability to commit to the challenge or expand their mind to accept that they may actually be able to pass Special Forces selection if they just applied themselves. These people exist in all professions and walks of life, and I'm not suggesting that there is anything wrong with being one of them. Society is made up of all kinds of people which allows for a bell curve to exist in any facet of life that you choose to scrutinise. Without those who are average in some area there can be no above-average people, no chance to excel in some facet of your life. You can bet that most people who excel at something truly suck at lots of other things, no one can be a boss at everything. I know lots of people who are living "average" lives and are perfectly happy doing so.

I observe them from a distance, and in many ways, I would love to be one of them. I would love to be able to wake up in the morning at 7am and be completely content with my existence, rather than getting up to an alarm at 5am to get a couple hours of hustle done before I head off to my day job. I'd love to be able to happily watch TV during the day on the weekend, remote in one hand, beer in the other. I can't however, for reasons I can't put a finger on I am just not wired that way. I have an inherent need to continually better myself in some tangible way; otherwise my self-worth is challenged. As stated above, there is nothing wrong with not having this internal drive, and living an "average" life, if you're comfortable with this and truly happy then that is great. My issue is with those who choose to live that life and then criticise others who are striving tirelessly to rise above average, especially in the context where it will have absolutely no bearing on their existence directly. These are the people who are toxic to your dreams and are the critics who do not count that Mr. Roosevelt was drawing reference to. On reflection, prior to becoming a doctor or joining Special Forces I never experienced hate from those who were already in the occupations that I aspired to, only encouragement. It seemed that both within the Special Forces and medical communities everyone I had dealings with was encouraging me to strive to join their organisations, and it was only those who were not qualified in any way, shape, or form to provide valid feedback that seemed to have issue with my aspirations.

I'm not suggesting that you should completely disregard criticism in all forms, and from all people. Criticism is an important tool that you can use to hold a mirror up to your dreams and thoroughly challenge whether they are the right ones for you. The right criticism from the right person may allow you to refine your goals in a productive manner, or perhaps realise that they are actually not the right goals for you at all. As tough a realisation as the latter can be to make, it is better to make it early in the pursuit of the wrong goal then waste valuable time and energy that could have been better spent in the pursuit of the right goal. My wife is the perfect person to critically review my dreams and as-pirations and believe me she is a harsh critic! While I don't always appreciate her honest opinion at the time, were it not for her frank criticism of some of my harebrained schemes I'm quite sure we would have been bankrupt several times over by now. The key here is that my wife's opinion is valid because I know she truly does have my best interests at heart. I know that once I commit to something she will back me in that endeavor no matter what, and most im-portantly I respect her opinion because I know she will be directly impacted by the outcomes of what I do. She is the exception to Mr Roosevelt's rule, she is the critic who *does* actually count and should be listened to. Aside from these key people in our lives, critics, such as the career advisor in the story above, do not count and energy should not be wasted dwelling on their opinions.

To quote another literary genius on the same topic I will

borrow a couple of lines from Rudyard Kipling's magnificent poem *If*. Once again, if you haven't come across this one, do yourself a favour and Google it. In the first passage of that poem Kipling writes:

> *If you can trust yourself when all men doubt you, but*
> *make allowance for their doubting to*

This couple of lines speaks to me on the topic of goals as well, but in a more inclusive way with regards to considering the opinion of others than just ignoring their criticism outright. When applied to the context of pursuing life goals, I relate Kipling's words here to backing yourself 100% to be able to achieve the goal you have set, however to not be completely and immediately dismissive of the opinion of others. Take their opinions on board and consider them, especially if those people are close to you and will be impacted by the pursuit of your goal, and if there's something productive to be gained from their opinion and doubt then use it, otherwise dismiss it after due consideration.

By far the best way to avoid criticism of your goals is to simply not broadcast them widely. Share them with those who need to know and only when they need to know them. Don't be the guy or girl who is always running their mouth about how they are going to do this or that. For the most part these are the people who will ultimately never attempt to pursue said goals, and if they do they are setting themselves up for an epic fall if they have widely publicised their pursuits and then fail to achieve them. It's best to hustle in silence and only pop up on the radar when absolutely necessary, and even then, let your actions do the talking rather than your words.

The Fight in the Dog

Another one of my all-time favorite quotes comes from the famous author Mark Twain and reads:

> *It's not the size of the of the dog in the fight, it's the size of the fight in the dog*

As a relatively short person myself and as already discussed weighing in at some meager 70-odd kilograms, this quote resonates with me tremendously. If there's one thing that I learned from a five-year involvement in Special Forces selection courses, initially as a candidate, and then as the doctor supporting them, it's not to underestimate the little bloke. Let me tell you a story to illustrate.

For as long as I can remember into my childhood I've been in the habit of psyching myself out in any competitive environment, convincing myself that everyone else around me was more highly trained, better prepared, and more naturally gifted than I was. I'm not sure where this inherent insecurity came from and I imagine it is quite common among most of us. While I believe that it is much better to be a little on the insecure side as opposed to overly self-assured, taken to extremes this insecurity can be debilitating on performance. As I moved into my late teenage years and started to find some success as a triathlete I began to realise the truth behind the Mark Twain quote mentioned above, that being that a small dog with plenty of fight in it could prevail against a larger dog that wasn't willing or able to fight as hard. I recall one particular triathlon where everything went to plan on the day and I had a win against a competitive field of athletes, some of which who stood a good foot or so taller than me at the time. I vividly recall standing on the podium receiving my first-place trophy and having both the second and third placed athletes standing taller than me despite being on lower podium steps on either side! After a further few similar experiences during my triathlon days I began to develop a little more confidence in myself to be able to compete against physically more impressive athletes, although that inherent self-doubt never left me completely.

A number of years on from my triathlon experience when I was on the officer component of my Special Forces selection course and I found myself right back there in the pit of self-doubt. I was completely out of my comfort zone, being an inexperienced army doctor lined up against dozens of experienced army infantry officers, many of whom had multiple operational tours of Iraq and some with experience commanding troops in battle. One of the activities that we were required to do was called "Rate your

Mate" and involved the 30 or so officers left on the course by that stage organising ourselves into what we decided was an order of best to worst candidate. As you could imagine there was a fair bit of ego involved in the upper echelon and even some physical jostling for the top positions. Officers got in all sorts of squabbles with one another to justify why they felt they were more deserving of a higher position than the man next to them. Surprisingly, some seemed quite comfortable to settle at the bottom end of the pecking order without a fight. I placed myself right in the middle of the group, plumb in the centre of the bell curve. When we had finished organising ourselves we were left in three groups of about 10, being a "top-dog" group, the middle group in which I was situated, and the "bottom" group of 10. What was interesting about this exercise was that the groups could have almost been allocated based on physical stature alone; with the top group exclusively the tall, muscular soldiers that the general public would envisage as what a Special Forces soldier would look like. The middle group was officers of average to below average height and build such as myself, and the "bottom" group was made up wiry, more insecure looking officers, with a couple of sets of coke-bottle glasses thrown in among them for good measure. As the course progressed one-by-one the officers from the top-dog group quit at a rate that far exceeded those from the bottom and middle group. When we reached the end of the grueling three-week course only one or two of the top group remained, with the majority of successful officers coming from the bottom group in the rate your mate exercise. This was a phenomenon that I continued to observe over many subsequent selection courses that I supported as a doctor, and after years of pondering it now makes perfect sense to me. You see the Alpha male top-dog soldiers who arrange themselves towards the pointy end of the pecking order are the types who have excelled throughout their lives, often on the sporting field, academically, and probably with the ladies. Things have come easily to them, and through a combination of genetics and natural talent they have often times been able to achieve at a high level with minimal to moderate levels of training or study. Society has held them in high esteem and their ego has been allowed to develop accordingly. In the army Special Forces selection scenario they have usually come from the elite elements of their regular army units, being either sniper or reconnaissance elements, and junior officers and soldiers alike look up to them. All of a sudden they find themselves on a course where they are treated like shit around the clock and everything they say or do is met with a barrage of humiliating abuse. Their competence is questioned at every opportunity and after every one of their efforts and exertions they are told they were not equal to the task. There is method to the madness behind the psychological barrage of the Special Forces selection process, but to the ego-driven top-dog soldier this situation is completely foreign and so overwhelmingly confronting that the majority of them cannot handle it and withdraw from the course at own request to return to the comfort of their previous units where their social status is already established.

In stark contrast to the top dogs are the soldiers who find themselves in the bottom ranks of the "rate your mate" type exercises. These are the ones who never excelled at anything in their youth, and for who any success in life has come entirely through sheer grit and dogged determination. They have forced their bodies and minds to transcend their genetic or social boundaries to excel in the face of what the universe appeared to have mapped out for them. Many have dug themselves out of the rut of lower socioeconomic disadvantage or a troubled upbringing to not only reach a level playing field with those around them but to show the world that despite their genetics and past that they can excel. Most will have been bullied to some degree at school, and you can guarantee they were never the cool kid. In my opinion it is likely that having been bullied places the chip on their shoulder and the fire in their belly to prove a point to those who bullied them by doing something exceptional with their lives. I suspect that either consciously or subconsciously the effect of that school bullying is what drives many of these people to be able to log the years of hard study, training, or both required to claw their way to the top. I use the military example because it is one I have witnessed first-hand an am familiar with, however these small dogs with extraordinary amounts of fight in them exist in all fields. For better or worse their pasts have made them accustomed to being put down and belittled, and rather than dissuade them this treatment simply strengthens their resolve towards their goals. They know that things will not come easily to them and they have accepted this, and if they persist and begin to see success in their life they start to realise that they can actually take on the bigger dogs and most times win.

Calvin Coolidge sums up eloquently what I'm trying to convey here with the following quote:

> *Nothing in this world can take the place of persistence. Talent will not: nothing is more common than unsuccessful men with talent. Genius will not; unrewarded genius is almost a proverb. Education will not: the world is full of educated derelicts. Persistence and determination alone are omnipotent.*

For an outstanding illustration of a small dog with superhuman amounts of fight, I recommend reading *The Crossroad* by Mark Donaldson VC. *The Crossroad* tells the story of Mark's journey from troubled youth, to the death of his father and unsolved presumed murder of his mother, to the army, Special Forces, and ultimately the actions that resulted in him being awarded Australia's highest honour for gallantry on the battlefield, The Victoria Cross for Australia. I'm humbled to call Mark a mate and his story epitomises the point I illustrate above.

Walking Down

There's a little known but hugely motivational passage that originates from a cult classic film from my childhood that, in my opinion, perfectly summates the act of dedicated goal setting, persistence, and pursuit of excellence. Sadly, I fear that it has been lost over the years and I feel a deep personal responsibility to revive it, as words as profound as these should not be lost to time. The movie is called *Colors* and it is a 1988 cop film set in the gritty ganglands of South Central Los Angeles. It stars Robert Duvall as a respected senior police officer and a young Sean Penn as a cocky, new to the job, hard-charging junior cop out to make his mark. In the particular scene I'm drawing reference to Duvall's character is using an analogy to explain his life philosophy to Penn's character by describing a scenario involving a young bull and an old bull standing atop a hill overlooking a paddock full of cows. The young bull turns to the old bull and says, "Hey Pop, let's say we run down there and fuck one of them cows", to which the old bull replies "No son. Let's walk down and fuck 'em all". How good is that? Do yourself a favour and look the film up, if for nothing else than to hear Duvall utter those words.

Once you move past the profanity and awesomeness of Duvall's character's philosophy, and really break it down, there are many profound lessons contained within. Superficially it reiterates the inherent difference in attitude between youth, particularly testosterone-fueled male youth, and older, wiser people in their approach to a challenge. Among all of us, but especially youth, there is often the desire to find a shortcut to an objective, a quick-fix, to "run down". Sure, you may actually have your way with a single cow in the end, but like putting a nice coat of icing on a poorly made cake, there's no substance beneath the success and no hard work backing it up as a platform for further success. I fear that modern day social media fuels the impression that the quick-fix success stories are possible. We have become so saturated with ten second snapshots of people doing extraordinary things day-in, day-out in our various feeds that we begin to think that this is the norm. What we don't get an appreciation for in those ten second snapshots are the thousands of hours of training that went into getting to the point that made the extraordinary ten seconds possible. We don't see the walking down. This leads to the popular culture tendency to believe that extraordinary is achievable somehow but provides absolutely no concept of how to do it because let's face it, the walking down part isn't sexy and certainly wouldn't grab our attention in the fraction of a second that we give it as we scroll through our feeds looking for a "thumb stopper" worthy of clicking on. These ten second snapshots provide us with absolutely no framework as to how the person came to be able to perform such amazing feats, no roadmap as to how the viewer may be able to reach the destination that the person performing the feat has reached. This subsequently leads to the assumption that the person achieving the feat is somewhat superhuman, with some freakish, unnatural power that allows them to be exceptional. This assumption then goes on to lead the viewer to conclude that because they are a "normal" person with no such superpower that they will forever be unable to achieve the exceptional, so they don't bother to try. At best they may run down and have a go at a single cow. What's missing from the picture is the "walking down" piece, the "ten thousand hours" if you subscribe to that theory of mastery (if you haven't heard of the 10,000 hour theory, look it up and see what you think). There is no place for this in our fast-paced, modern day consumption of information through social media for the simple fact that it is not shiny. We love to watch professional sport and marvel at the excellence on display, but no one would tune in to watch an athlete perform ten thousand hours of training over a period of years or decades. It's easy to fall into the trap of watching a professional tennis player winning a Grand Slam, or a professional golfer winning a Green Jacket and be unable to comprehend that they have just earned millions of dollars in prize money for a few hours work. What we might fail to recognise in these instances is that it is not the few hours we have just watched that they are being remunerated for; it is the endless hours of training over countless years that is being reimbursed. The early mornings, the endless struggles, the injuries, blood, sweat and tears. I'm quite certain that if you stacked up most professional sports peoples' earnings against the hours spent getting to that point that their average wage would be less than that earned for flipping burgers for an equivalent number of hours. It is the classic example of only taking twenty years to become an overnight success, these exceptional people have taken the time to walk down and only pop up on our social media radar at the point when they are having their way with the whole herd of cows. In his outstanding book *Outliers*, Malcolm Gladwell analyses the makings of some of the most successful people in the world from varied disciplines and drills down into the "walking down" that led them to become so amazing. If you have an interest in the area and haven't come across *Outliers* I urge you get a copy and have a read. While you're at it grab his entire back catalogue and read those books as well, the man is a genius!

The military equivalent to the sporting examples provided above is the murky grey world of Special Forces. Once again popular media would have you believe that these units are full of 8-foot-tall super-soldiers who can leap buildings in single bounds and kill enemy with their bare hands. Owing somewhat to operational security consider-ations, as well as falling victim to the ADHD world of social media ten second engagements, Special Forces units are viewed by many as another unobtainable elite pinnacle of society reserved for those with special powers that only a lucky few have bestowed upon them. The media lets us in on certain events such as Operation Neptune Spear, being the incredible raid into Pakistan conducted by US Naval Special Warfare elements and resulting in the demise of Osama Bin Laden. What we don't see there is the cumulative decades of training that went into preparing every one of the members involved in all facets of that operation, be it on the ground, flying the helicopters, or behind the scenes planning, that allowed the mission to be such an incredible success. Once again, we see the end result, but not the walking down. Further perpetuating the mystique of Special Forces are mottos such as that shared by both the British and Australian Special Air Service Regiments "Who Dares Wins". This motto in isolation suggests that anyone with enough daring can win, but this is of course for the most part untrue. If any old bunch of daring but inappropriately trained blokes had jumped on helicopters and landed in Bin Laden's back yard I'm sure the outcome of Neptune Spear would have been significantly different. "Who Dares Wins" comes with the caveat that those daring actions that result in a win rely on those performing them to have been mentally and physically sharpened through years to decades of training, and then appropriately supported by an administrative and logistical support systems that enable them to perform at the level required to win through daring. This leads me to another popular catchphrase being "The Tip of the Spear" which in the military context is often used to describe the door-kicking operators at the pointy end of Special Forces units. This analogy is very appropriate for these groups of men and sometimes women, as it is the tip of the spear that projects forward and interfaces with the enemy in its literal application. A razor-sharp spear tip will do more damage than a blunt one, and requires a significant degree of sharpening, as do the members of Special Forces units. Equally as relevant to the real-world spear tip however, is the fact that in isolation a spear tip is a fundamentally useless piece of metal without the remainder of the spearhead, a solid attachment to the spear handle, and the handle itself. Even then, the sharpest, most perfectly crafted spear by itself is also useless without being in the hands of an appropriately mentally and physically trained warrior to employ it on the field of battle. My point being, while we all celebrate the tip of the spear, we should never lose site of the other 95% of the overall apparatus that makes the tip what it is. The less shiny roles behind the pointy end deserve our acknowledgement and respect equally, if not more than those at the pointy end. In the military environment, these are the elements that insert and extract soldiers from the target, those who maintain the aircraft or vehicles that perform that role, those who feed the soldiers, maintain their weapons, plan the missions, organise all the logistics and so forth. Extending further back are the crews who fly and maintain the aircraft that move the units strategically from their National Support Base, to the general public who receives the soldiers when they get home, and last but very not least to the families of the deployed soldiers who maintain the home front and ensure bills are paid, kids are fed and bathed, and everyone makes it to school and soccer practice while mum or dad are deployed. It's important that in our admiration of the Tip of The Spear in any facet of life that we also give due respect to the years of effort that go into creating it and to the extensive support network behind it. In another similar civilian analogy, we all love a good rock band front man and lead guitarist, but most of us can never name the bass player or drummer of our favorite band. Without these talented musicians towards the back of the stage the music would probably be nowhere near as impressive. The obvious exception to this rule is Dave Grohl, that guy is 100% legit and I suspect could rock out solo equally as well as when he's fronting the Foo Fighters.

Eating an Elephant

Given that our modern-day social media world doesn't provide us the framework as to how to reach excellence, let's take the opportunity to explore the goal setting required to get there. There are all sorts of motivational quotes about goal setting, many of which draw reference to the need for a map of some description to be able to arrive at your destination. The analogy of a car trip is often used and is a good one, without planning out the towns you need to go through on the road trip to your destination then how do you know if you're headed in the right direction? Likewise, there are all sorts of motivational passages about getting started on the journey, including things like a journey of a thousand miles starts with a single step, or a raging river starts with a single drop. My favorite has always been the following:

How do you eat an elephant? One bite at a time!

I was at the zoo with my family just weeks prior to writing this book and found myself thinking of this goal setting analogy as I looked up at a huge elephant in an enclosure in front of me. It got me wondering what the goal setting process would actually look like to literally eat an elephant. I once read an article about a French bloke by the name of Michel Lotito who ate a plane over a period of years by filing down every one of the metal components and eating them bit-by-bit. For the rubber and interior bits, he boiled them until they were soft enough to ingest and consumed them also. I remember being struck by a couple of thoughts at the time, firstly why is this man not receiving the mental health support that he requires for his obvious issues, but secondly what a remarkable example of goal setting and accomplishment. It took him two years, but he stuck with it and got there in the end. Allegedly when the Guinness Book of Records presented him with a plaque for his remarkable effort he ate that as well!

Before we get back to the elephant example I'd like to touch on some of the popular theory behind goal setting. Most readers will be familiar with the concept of SMART goals, if you're not and you're interested, Google it. As a quick recap the acronym stands for following:

S – Specific
M – Measureable
A – Achievable
R – Realistic
T – Time limited

There are a few different variants on these exact terms,

but the principles remain the same. SMART goals are all about better defining and putting some boundaries on our goals in order to give them structure and assist in working towards achieving them. Let's look at the individual components and elaborate a little.

Specific – it's important to specify exactly what your goal is so you know when you've achieved it. For example, goals such as getting "skinny" or "fit" are quite vague and subject to interpretation, however a goal to lose 10 kilograms or to run a five-minute mile are well defined and specific.

Measurable – you need some metric to be able to measure your progress against, for example "I want to be a better person" is difficult to measure, however "I want to volunteer 10 hours a month at a homeless shelter" is measurable against a metric of time.

Achievable – I'm all about setting difficult goals for myself that push me out of my comfort zone and keep me moving forward, however it's important to make sure that they are tangibly achievable. Setting unachievable goals over the long run will just lead to constant failure and eventual disillusionment and potential quitting. When I was training up for Special Forces selection I knew that the goal was going to be a difficult one for me to achieve, but by the same token I also knew that people just like me had accomplished it and if I worked hard enough it was achievable for me as well.

On the flip side though as an example, as a 40 plus year old now it would be unachievable for me to get on the Olympic swim team, that horse has well and truly bolted (if it was ever there!).

Realistic – this one sounds obvious, but it is what differentiates tangible goals from pipe dreams. Once again it is great to set yourself challenging goals, however if they're unrealistic then you are likely to meet with the same fate as those who set unachievable goals. For example, for me to set the goal of becoming the President of the USA would be unrealistic. For one I'm not a US citizen and I was not born there. Furthermore, even if I did meet the citizenship eligibility requirements I have no political or personal background to use as a platform to reach that high office.

Time limited – You need to set an end point for when to achieve your goal by. Some time limits are already defined, such as completing an organised marathon or other sporting event on a specific day; others require you to define a timeframe. Setting a time limit for your goals is a powerful thing to do as it starts a stopwatch ticking to get the goal achieved and holds you accountable.

Once you've set your SMART goal you can then break it down into manageable sub-goals, set time limits on those and start your journey towards summiting the mountain of your larger goal. For example, if your goal is to lose 12kg of weight in a six-month period then you could break that down into sub-goals of losing 2kg a month or 500g a week. The weight loss may not be as linear as those sub-goals require, however it gives you the roadmap along the way to your end goal to monitor your progress. Another powerful tool in goal setting is to write your goal down and stick it somewhere you will see it regularly. The simple act of physically writing the goal out is a strong motivator for most people as all of a sudden you are acknowledging it as real and strengthening your resolve towards it. Seeing the written goal regularly serves to reinforce this resolve and keep you motivated towards the end result, particularly on days where you seem to be moving away from your goal rather than towards it. The setting of small sub-goals week-in, week-out allows you to start making tangible progress in the right direction and provides the positive reinforcement of ticking off the sub-goals as you go along and experiencing the satisfaction involved with that achievement. Whether or not you share your goal with other people comes back to the points discussed earlier and depends as to whether you feel those people are likely to add positive or negative energy to your aspirations. Ultimately in order to achieve ambitious goals in life the vast majority of the inspiration and motivation required needs to be derived from within, and very little should be required from external sources, so if you feel that you're relying on someone else to push you towards your goal then maybe it isn't the right goal for you or maybe you don't want it as badly as you initially thought.

With all of that in mind let's turn back to the *How do you eat an elephant* question and for the sake of the exercise break that down into a SMART goal. One last point before we kick off is that SMART goals don't necessarily need to be written start to finish, you can jump around between the different categories as you go along the goal defining process.

Let's be perfectly clear here, I have no intention of ever eating elephant and I don't condone the behavior, however hypothetically was I to want to eat an elephant my first question would be to assess if it is an *Achievable* goal. Is elephant meat edible for a start and if so where in the world are they still eating it? After a little online research, it turns out that elephant meat is well and truly edible, has been eaten by man since the beginning of time, and is still getting eaten regularly in a few countries of Central Africa. I am not a vegetarian, so therefore I can now tick off the Achievable category of my SMART goal and move on.

I think Realistic would be the next category to logically move onto in this scenario. In my current life situation, I have a fulltime job in Australia, a wife, three kids in school, all the usual bills and a mortgage. My wife would obviously need to buy-in to my goal; otherwise I would likely be eating my elephant as a middle-aged single man! Having ascertained that to eat my elephant I would be required to move to Central Africa for a period of time I would need to analyse the logistics of that. I would need to consider the financial implications of the goal, to fund my family in Australia as well as my elephant-eating lifestyle in Africa,

I would need to quit my job or take a significant period of leave, and so on and so forth. I'd need to consider my safety in the specific Central African country I chose, the visa process for entering the country, where specifically I might live, the local language spoken, and establishing relationships to facilitate access to elephant meat. While all of these factors present hurdles themselves and may lead to sub-goals on the way to eating an elephant, they are important to consider in detail and will inform other categories of the SMART goal process. During this phase of goal setting it might be possible to start thinking laterally of opportunities that could assist in your goal attainment. For example, given that eating an elephant is an unusual and unorthodox goal, it may be that it could attract sponsorship of some description potentially to create a documentary, which may offset some of the financial burden of the goal.

Now that eating an elephant has been deemed Achievable and assuming I've managed to get my wife's approval and mapped out potential solutions to the financial and logistical challenges presented to make it Realistic, it's time to drill down into the Specifics and Measurability of the goal. An important question to answer at this stage is exactly what do I mean by eating an elephant? Am I referring to the meat only, or am I talking about eating the entire beast: eyeballs, toenails, internal organs, bones, tusks, skin and all! This comes down to the Specifics of the goal and it can be seen that they're very important to define. If my goal is to eat the entirety of the animal, it creates a whole different set of challenges than if I define my goal as eating only the meat. I would need to consider a way to grind down and eat all the bones, as well as boil up the tough elephant skin to turn it into something edible. Now if a man can eat a plane as previously mentioned, then surely the entire elephant goal is still in the realms of Achievable, but significantly more difficult than the meat-only alternative. Let's go with the meat-only option for the purposes of this exercise. Next question to ask is how much meat exactly is on an elephant? The answer to this according to Wikipedia is around 1000 pounds or 450 kilograms. Defining this figure makes the goal Measurable and provides the opportunity to start working out rough timeframes that it is likely to take to achieve our goal, as naturally there is going to be a limit as to how much meat I could realistically ingest in a single day. Furthermore, in better defining the specifics of the goal it would need to be considered whether the meat all needed to come from a single elephant, or whether it was acceptable to more simply eat the equivalent weight of elephant meat that would add up to an entire elephant. If the goal were defined as the former it would introduce a range of storage and refrigeration logistics that wouldn't exist in the latter. Let's go with the latter in this exercise.

Now that we have defined the Specifics of the goal and made it Measureable, we can better define the Time limits to place on it. Once again, a quick scrub of the Internet suggests that the average middle-class western adult male eats somewhere in the vicinity of 100kg of meat a year. At that rate it would take four and a half years to hit my goal of eating the equivalent of an elephant in meat. This might be an acceptable rate if my intention was to move my family to Central Africa for a few years and chip away at my goal slowly, however if my plan was to go solo and smash out my goal then I would need to step up the ingestion rate significantly. Realistically I reckon I could consistently eat around 1kg of meat daily for a sustained period, give or take, and doing the math on that figure would get me to the goal at the 450-day mark, or around 15 months. Assuming that there will be some days where I don't hit the 1kg mark, or simply can't face up to yet another elephant steak, let's stretch that out to 18 months to be on the safe side.

Right, now let's have a look at that goal in entirety. While the calculations suggest it would technically only take a year and a half of eating time to complete, the overall goal would take more like 3-5 years minimum to accomplish. The initial phase would consist of all the pre-planning, research, money saving, and perhaps even a reconnaissance visit or two to Central Africa for a look around the various countries where elephant is eaten and have a taste test to make sure it's palatable enough. During the preparation years I could start to increase my meat consumption at home and do trial periods where I consistently ate 1kg of meat a day to see how it went and to condition my body to deal with it. Month-in, month-out during the preparation phase of the goal I could set sub-goals of researching recipes for elephant meat, potentially learn local customs and the language of the Central African location I'd chosen, and other such sub-goals towards better preparing for the ultimate goal.

While this is a ridiculous example to use I feel that it illustrates the components of a long-term ambitious SMART goal nicely. To anyone standing in a zoo looking up at an elephant the thought of eating it seems overwhelmingly impossible, however once you sit down and deconstruct the goal you can begin to see that it may actually be achievable if you plan for it and are willing to make the sacrifices to make it happen. The same can be said for any SMART goal in life, because by definition they are inherently achievable and realistic if you have gone through the process of defining them properly. It took me over six years from the time I set myself the goal of attempting Special Forces selection to when I finally had the chance to get on the course, and in the beginning the goal seemed as daunting as eating an elephant. Through defining a SMART goal and then creating smaller time-limited sub-goals, I was slowly able to move towards my objective and eventually eat that elephant one bite at a time.

The Elusive Sandy Beret

Having gone to great lengths to break down the SMART goal setting process and illustrating the fact that lofty goals are achievable if approached in the right manner and with due persistence, now I'm going to tell you that achieving the end goal may not actually matter in the slightest! Let me share a story with you to illustrate my point.

In the world of military Special Forces the act of becoming *beret-qualified* or *badged* signifies your arrival into the clan; the achievement of your goal to join the unit you've strived to be a part of. The individual beret of a unit is its identifier, and within some units different coloured berets designate different levels of training and accomplishment. In the SAS it is the Sandy Beret that signifies a soldier who has successfully completed all the requisite courses to become "qualified". It is quite rightly held in high esteem as to join the ranks of these remarkable soldiers requires years of dedicated training and is a significant accomplishment. I can recall vividly the night that the light bulb came on in my mind that I wanted to become a beret-qualified doctor with the Australian SASR. I had been at a barbeque with a group of SASR operators and in discussion with a couple of them it came out that I was on an army scholarship at the time to become a doctor. I had given little to no thought to joining Special Forces prior to that point and at that stage probably didn't even realise that the option of being a doctor with Special Forces existed. During the conversation on that night one of the operators suggested to me that I should do selection and join SASR, which I initially dismissed completely citing the fact that I was on a trajectory to become a doctor with the army. The operator continued, "Yeah, that's what I mean, do selection and become a beret-qualified doctor with the unit". The light bulb flicked on and I immediately had a new focus to my very existence, I was going to be a beret-qualified doctor with SASR.

There are many hurdles to becoming beret-qualified with the SASR, the first truly significant one of which is the grueling three-week selection course. As previously mentioned it took me over six years from the night of that barbeque to finally toe the starting line of the SASR selection course, and I filled that time by setting and hitting sub-goals towards preparation for selection. The three-week course came and went, and I was still standing at the end of it (albeit only just) and was considered suitable for ongoing training with SASR. This was an excellent result, however represented only the initial step toward the accomplishment of being a beret-qualified doctor with SASR. To achieve the ultimate goal, I was required to successfully complete a series of courses known as the Reinforcement Cycle (Reo), designed to equip a soldier with the base skill set to be competent in the role as an operator with the unit. Here's where my dream got a little sidetracked. You see, I had been due to deploy a few months after the selection course with the army unit I had come from at the time, and unable to replace the doctor for the trip I was recalled to my original unit to deploy. This had been the agreement I made with the Commanding Officer of the unit at the time and was not altogether unexpected, however was disappointing nonetheless. Even if I hadn't missed Reo because of the requirement to deploy, it turned out that I had contracted a significant infection in one of my knees during the selection course that ultimately needed surgical drainage followed by a period of hospitalisation and then a couple of months of intravenous antibiotics to resolve, which would have certainly bumped me off the Reo course anyway. My knee healed well enough to deploy on operations with my original unit and on return from that tour I posted to one of Australia's other premier Special Forces units in a holding pattern of sorts prior to plugging back in with the SASR Reo Cycle of the selection course the following year. Although this would mean that I would have to complete the Reo courses with a cohort that weren't the ones I did selection with, assuming I was successful on the courses it would allow me to achieve my goal of becoming beret-qualified. What happened then was an opportunity to deploy as the doctor with the Australian Special Operations Task Group to Afghanistan, which I took and once again caused me to miss Reo cycle the following year. The theme continued for the next year and by the year following, when I finally got across to SASR there had been a change of guard and the new hierarchy no longer supported my desire to complete Reo and become beret-qualified. I had picked up enough courses along the way to make me competent in my role and I was doing the job I was assigned to do, both domestically and in the deployed setting. It was therefore assessed at the time that Reo was going to take me away from my primary role as the unit doctor for a period of up to a year without really adding any value to my employability. I remember being furious at the time as this decision represented the crushing of my ultimate goal of becoming a beret-qualified doctor with SASR, a goal that I had worked towards for over eight years by that stage. The show went on however and there was no time to sulk with regular high-tempo tours of Afghanistan and Counter-Terrorism duties among other commitments when not deployed.

My time with Australian Special Forces flew past and came to an end after five years and four tours of Afghanistan with the Special Operations Task Group. In between my operational tours I had the opportunity to spend time on exercise and with training teams in other far-flung regions of both Australia and the world, as well as represent our medical capability in the USA on several occasions and to NATO Special Operations in Belgium. It had been an incredibly privileged period of time and on reflection the colour of my beret had absolutely no bearing on the job I did over the years. I can't think of a single instance where having completed Reo and accomplished my original goal of becoming beret-qualified would have altered the trajectory of my career in the slightest.

Ultimately, in the end I failed to achieve the goal I had set out to achieve, the goal that had motivated me for well over a decade. What I came to realise however was that the achievement of my original goal turned out to be completely inconsequential, and I managed to accomplish everything I wanted to in my military medical career without ever wearing that elusive Sandy Beret. Of course, without setting the goal of becoming beret-qualified in the first instance I never would have started on the trajectory that took me to where I eventually ended up, so it was critical to have that goal to strive towards, it just didn't matter in the end that I never achieved it. My point is this: it is setting the goal and then striving towards it that truly matters. In the end whether you hit the goal or not, the simple act of moving towards it and accomplishing sub-goals along the way may prove just as, if not more, satisfying than the original goal itself.

Turns Out I Sucked at Triathlon

The purpose of this chapter is to address the topic of failure and look at it from a couple of different angles. The Internet is full of motivational passages, often accompanied by an early morning silhouette of someone summiting a mountain, that would have you believe that any goal is achievable if you just keep trying and don't accept failure as an option. For the most part I do believe this to be true, particularly if you've constructed a legitimate SMART goal that by definition has been assessed as being realistic and achievable. Having said that there can be a fine line between pursuing your goal to the ends of the Earth and simply flogging a dead horse. I'm not suggesting for a second that you should give up easily as soon as the path towards your goal becomes difficult, to borrow another inspirational line from Roosevelt's "The Man in The Arena" *There is no effort without erring and shortcoming*, however by the same token you do need to know when to quit. A good example of this scenario is the story of my epic failure to achieve my first real life goal.

As a kid I had absolutely no desire to join the military or to become a doctor. From my late teens onward my sole life goal was to become a professional triathlete at the expense of everything else. I moved my life to the epicenter of triathlon in Australia at the time and maneuvered myself onto one of the premier training squads in the country. Around the same time, I vividly recall attending key parades at Australia's Royal Military College where my best mate was undergoing officer training and watching on bemused as he and his cohort marched around in perfect clean-cut unison on the parade ground. I had long hair, shaved legs, and an earring at the time and military life was about as foreign a concept as I could have imagined. As for becoming a doctor, the thought had never crossed my mind. My grades from high school were nowhere near good enough to even consider applying for medical school, and it wouldn't have mattered even if they were because I was destined to make my millions as a professional triathlete anyway! I had enrolled in part-time university only as a means to garner the support of my Aunt and parents who had agreed to help me out financially on the proviso that I studied something.

For my initial years as a junior triathlete I showed some promise, occasionally making my way onto the podium in races here and there. As the years went by and I moved past the junior ranks however what early promise I had shown started to evaporate. Despite doing the exact same training as some of the best triathletes in the world I was simply not even in the same league as them. Rather than trying to compete head-to-head with them I started scheduling my races around where the best athletes would be in order to stand a chance at achieving a decent position in smaller second tier events. I was giving it my all and the dream was starting to unravel. By the time I was in my early twenties and had been chasing my triathlon goals for about five years straight I could see clearly that I was not going to be anywhere near as good as I had wanted to be. Younger generations of athletes were coming through and despite being several years my junior were starting to beat me. Furthermore, I had accumulated a couple of niggling injuries that would flare periodically and force me to miss valuable training, further hampering my aspirations. I foresaw my future in triathlon as plodding along the same path for the subsequent decade or so, chasing scraps of prize money here and there at obscure events where the top pros weren't bothering to race, before eventually scraping together enough money to potentially open a bike shop or start a coaching company. There were several examples of exactly that guy in the squad I was training with, getting by with low-level sponsorships, traveling the world here and there to race, but never actually competing on the world stage as such. There was absolutely nothing wrong with that lifestyle, in fact it looked relatively appealing, it just wasn't my dream. I had been doing everything that I could towards my goal and as it turned out it was simply out of reach.

That led me to face up to an important process in itself, and that is to revisit and review your goals periodically and make sure that they still meet the SMART criteria. Although I have no recollection of setting a SMART goal per se for my triathlon ambitions, as an 18-year-old who was showing some promise in triathlon at the time, a career in professional triathlon was both achievable and seemingly realistic to me. People were doing it, why couldn't I? Five years on and I found myself a 23-year-old who had devoted five years to fulltime training and racing in triathlon and was harbouring a couple of injuries, all of a sudden the reality of my goal was slipping away from me and it was looking less achievable to hit my desired target. I could have continued on my pathway, but it was no longer headed where I wanted. I had followed the correct steps to get to my goal but just couldn't seem to get there, the end destination of where I was headed by that point was something completely different and was no longer for me. My choices at that stage in my life were to compromise and continue on along my path, or to make the tough decision to accept that I had done my very best and that my goal was no longer realistic or achievable. I did the latter, and while it was a tough realisation at the time and left me directionless for a period of nearly a year, it freed me up to open my mind to other possible goals to pursue which ultimately led me to applying for both medical school and the army. Both were goals that I had never even considered prior to that point, and goals that I wouldn't have considered had I chosen to compromise and continue on my triathlon path that was no longer leading to the professional career that I had initially hoped.

The point of this story is that it's important to periodically review your long-term goals and reassess them against the SMART criteria. Most references to failure in the motivational literature redefine it as another opportunity in disguise, or a speed hump along the way to your goal. Indeed, there are many famous instances where great people have failed seemingly endless times before hitting their goals. Thomas Edison springs to mind here, who is rumoured to have made over 1000 failed attempts at a light bulb before his final revolutionary success, or J.K. Rowling who was allegedly knocked back countless times before her Harry Potter series of books were finally accepted for publication. The difference between these examples and me quitting on my triathlon goal is that inventing light bulbs and pursuing book publication aren't necessarily linked to peak physical condition. Naturally both of these brilliant people would have made endless sacrifices in their pursuit of their eventual success, however there was unlikely an absolute reason why their goal had ceased to be realistic and achievable. Certainly never quit on a life goal too easily, and if you reassess your goals periodically as you pursue them and they continue to remain realistic and achievable then temporary failures are just small roadblocks that must be overcome. If, however your assessment is that your goals have slipped from being realistic and achievable your options are to compromise and head in the new direction that your journey is taking you or accept failure in that particular goal and set a new SMART goal to devote your energy towards.

Leap and the Net Will Appear

I love the saying *leap and the net will appear* and can think of a few good examples in my life where I've leapt without a net and one did actually appear! It's amazing how once you commit to something, particularly something big, that the universe provides a net, or you're forced to hustle like a madman to make one appear. The best example of mine to illustrate this point is the story of how I came to own a Lamborghini. To appreciate this story fully the reader needs to understand that I am fanatical about cars, and especially classic Italian cars. Like many boys of my age I grew up with posters of the Lamborghini Countach and Ferrari Testarossa on my walls and had a matchbox car collection of the same marques, as well as Lancias, Lotus' and similar classic sports cars, but it was the Lamborghinis that I was particularly drawn to. I loved everything about the cars and the company, especially the legend that Ferruccio Lamborghini had started making cars only after a heated discussion with Enzo Ferrari about how Ferrari might be able to improve their gearboxes. Allegedly Enzo told Lamborghini, who was at the time a wealthy tractor manufacturer and owner of Ferrari cars, that if he thought he could do better than he should build a car himself. And that's exactly what he did, founding Automobili Lamborghini in 1963 and the company taking it to Ferrari on the road ever since. During my early twenties I was working part time in hospitality and would often finish work in the early hours of the morning after cleaning up and closing the bar. Just a short deviation from my drive home was a Supercar dealership and most nights I'd park out the front and get out to gawk through the windows at the latest Lamborghinis on display. On occasion I'd go to the same dealership during opening hours to take a closer look at the mystical beasts.

Fast-forward again a number of years to 2009 and I had just started at my first Army Special Forces unit and had been immediately assigned to Domestic Counter Terrorist (DCT) duties. At the time I was driving a classic British sports car when one Saturday morning an Internet advertisement caught my eye. It was for a 1974 Lamborghini Urraco at a local dealership and was priced relatively cheaply for such a car. Ignoring the *beware the cheap Lamborghini* alarm that was going off in my mind I decided that I would take a drive down to the dealership and have a look at the car. I told my wife what I was doing, assured her I had no intention of buying the car and was simply going for a look, and hopped in my car to head off. As I was backing my car out of the garage I heard a banging on the bonnet of my car and turned to find my wife trying to get my attention to tell me something. I wound down my window to hear her say "don't you buy that fucking car!" It was as though she knew before I did that I was going to buy the car, but at that stage I can honestly say that my intentions, at least my conscious ones, were simply to go and have a look. I reassured my wife and continued on my way. The very second I approached the dealership and caught a glimpse of the gleaming red Lamborghini for sale I immediately knew that I had to buy that car. I went in and met the dealer, took the Lambo for a test drive, and despite it being a little under power and I suspected in need of an engine rebuild I put a deposit on it then and there with my credit card. I had no savings, my wife and I had just maxed out our borrowing capacity to buy an investment property, I was on a relatively average army wage that was only just covering our mortgages and bills, and I had put the deposit for the car on credit having promised my wife that I would not buy it. I had leapt with absolutely no net in sight and no idea how I was going to get one in place before I splatted into the ground. As I drove home I felt that sick feeling that you get in the pit of your gut when you've done something terribly wrong. I even phoned my parents and brother and explained the situation to them in an attempt to get advice on how to break the news to my wife. They all agreed that I was in big trouble and that the best approach was to confess immediately to my wife and put my head on the chopping board and hope for a clean cut. I took the less manly approach of waiting until the next day before telling my wife when we had visitors. I figured that the presence of others would serve to minimise her explosion at the news or at the very least provide witnesses to the assault that might very likely result shortly afterwards. She took the news exactly as expected and her initial outright fury eventually simmered down into a heated discussion of how on Earth we were going to be able to afford it, which was an excellent question. Further complicating the situation was the fact that the very next morning I was due out before dawn to get on a Navy ship and head off down the east coast of Australia to do some Counter-Terrorist training known as Ship Underway Recovery (SUR) training. As the name suggests, SUR involves learning to assault moving ships that have been taken by hostile forces, with the two primary means of boarding the ship being to fast rope onto it from a hovering helicopter or climb up a narrow, flexible caving ladder fired up from a jet boat in the water next to the ship and attached by a grappling hook. For the next week I found myself in between SUR serials on a satellite phone to the car dealership and various finance organisations frantically trying to convince them to lend me money for the car. Where there's a will there's a way, and I eventually cobbled together enough money through a combination of squeezing a bit of extra money out of our home loans, and two separate loans with the kind of lenders that charge 20% interest and are more likely to turn up at your doorstep with a baseball bat than a clipboard if you default. It was certainly not ideal, but I had secured the money to buy my Lamborghini, the next trick would be paying it off.

As soon as I returned from the SUR exercise I signed up for extra weekend shifts at a civilian medical clinic to help pay down the loans. Week days would be spent in my army role, looking after the Special Operators and spending a healthy amount of time at the range or swinging out of helicopters, and then on weekends I would spend long days looking after little Johnny's ingrown toenail or Aunty Flo's urinary incontinence every time she sneezed. It was a busy period, but I was able to pay off the high interest loans quickly before they got on top of me and then a deployment with the army took care of the rest of the loan and within 18 months I owned the Lamborghini outright, including paying for a sickeningly expensive engine and gearbox rebuild along the way!

My wife has always hated the car and in the decade that I've owned it I could count on a single hand the amount of times she's been in it. She does however appreciate how much it means to me and how much joy it has brought me over the years. On a positive the boom in classic car prices since I purchased the car has ironically made it unintentionally one of the best investments I have ever made, which is a point that I of course bring up often with my wife!

With hindsight the act of buying the car was impulsive and was truly an example of leaping without any idea if a net would appear or not. The purchase was made with emotion rather than any real calculated thought, and fortunately it worked out well. Reflecting on what might have happened, the worst case would probably have been that I couldn't get the finance to secure the car and had to pull out of the deal in the first place, perhaps losing my deposit if I did. Assuming I had gotten to the finance point and then wasn't able to pay the loan down then the solution would have been to sell the car, pay off what I could of the loans and then chip away at any remaining debt if the sale price didn't clear it. That would have been a tough lesson to learn and disappointing, but far from the end of the world.

The point of this story is that if there's something in life that you desperately want but you just can't quite map out a plan to get it, sometimes going all-in and leaping towards your objective is a powerful motivator to creating the net to land safely on. It may be that instead of a net appearing that a Wing Suit appears and steers you towards a slightly different destination than you originally thought, which is still a better outcome than staying on the ledge looking down at your dream and never having the courage to jump.

RAK On!

I'm a massive fan of the contemporary movement of Random Acts of Kindness (RAK). I believe there's a certain satisfaction that you get from performing a selfless act for someone else without any expectation of something in return that's hard, if not impossible, to get from other means. There are a couple of great mantras that come to mind when I think of RAK, the first of which comes from John Bunyan and reads:

> *You have not lived today until you have done something for someone who can never repay you.*

The second great passage that springs to mind when I think about the topic of RAK is the poem *Have You Earned Your Tomorrow* by Edgar Guest, which opens with the line *Is anybody happier because you passed his way?* and closes with:

> *As you close your eyes in slumber do you think that God would say,*

you have earned one more tomorrow by the work you did today?

By work in this poem Guest is referring to selfless efforts to help those around us, rather than self-serving acts with expectation of reward or favour.

With hindsight my dad, who was a very kind and generous man, exposed me to RAK from the earliest age. While we were never flush with cash growing up we certainly had plenty to get by and Dad never hesitated to share when he could. I vividly recall multiple occasions when Dad would pick up hitchhikers on long highway trips and when he dropped them off would often give them all the cash he had in his wallet at the time simply because he knew that they needed it more than he did. Sometimes the hitchhikers would try and make a plan to repay the money or attempt to get Dad's details, which Dad would always decline, suggesting that they could potentially repay the favour to someone else in need in the future. Dad was paying it forward long before that movement became famous! Having grown up with this kind of role model it was natural for me to fall into the habit of giving my money and time to those in need when I was in a position to do so. Don't get me wrong, I'm no Mother Teresa but if I have a few extra bucks in my pocket as I walk past a homeless person I will always give it to them. I know that many readers will be having the thought *well he probably just bought booze or drugs with it*, and you're right he may well have, but that doesn't diminish the act of giving and should never be a disincentive for generosity in these situations. What someone does with the money after I give it to them is completely outside of my control, but what *are* well within my control are the giving part and the amount given.

Another great life experience that I had in my early twenties that I believe played significantly into my current view on RAK and generosity in broader terms, was working in hospitality. I truly believe that every young person should have the humbling experience of waiting tables, working behind a bar, or an equivalent job, to truly learn about human nature. I had the added bonus of waiting tables and working behind the bar at a fairly fancy restaurant in a ritzy strip on the Gold Coast in Queensland Australia, which at the time was a hot spot where newly-rich folk in white leather shoes congregated to compare Supercars, trophy brides, and fancy watches. It was a real eye opener and while there were a handful of good people among those I served, for the most part they treated me like dirt, and to them I was nothing more than a minor inconvenience that stood between them and their meal or their next $25 top-shelf whisky. Sometimes they would actually tip me very well, but it always seemed to be done in a condescending manner that made me feel like they pitied me, and most times done as a grandiose gesture after they had made sure that everyone else at the table who they were clearly trying to impress were watching. It was an excellent insight into everything I never wanted to be when I finally started to earn some real money. The real kicker came when I had been accepted into medical school and I was coming to the end of my time working at the restaurant. Once word got out that I was going to be a doctor things changed completely and many of them actually took the time to talk to me, as if somehow I was all of a sudden someone worthy of their attention rather than just the bar guy. This only further solidified my opinion of those people and strengthened my resolve to never, ever become like them.

One RAK ritual that I have established stems from my childhood and the pure joy that I experienced when I got my first bike. I can remember it vividly, it was my 8th birthday and I got a blue and yellow BMX. With hindsight now, 8 is kind of old to be getting started riding bikes, but anyway that's just how it was! I was absolutely hooked and took to the bike with a passion that I'd never had for anything prior. I recall falling and getting back on repeatedly until I finally got the hang of riding, and then I recall the feeling of speed and pure freedom that came with riding a bike properly for the first time. Bikes became a huge part of my life for decades to come after that and I ended up riding hundreds of thousands of kilometers in my triathlon days but that initial experience has stayed with me. I even recall pretending to be sick on the Monday after my eighth birthday weekend so that I got get the day off school, and once my parents had gone to work getting out and riding my bike up and down the street for the whole day (yes that was back in the days when you left your sick 8-year-old home by themselves!).

Because of the profound impact that my first bike had on me, now every Christmas I buy a bike and a helmet for the Wishing Tree set up at a local department store, which is an initiative designed to donate gifts to anonymous children from financially disadvantaged backgrounds who may otherwise go without presents at Christmas. As my means have improved so has the quality of the bikes, but it's always a BMX and it's always addressed to an anonymous 8-year-old boy. The bike costs maybe a couple of hundred bucks, but the feeling of satisfaction that I get from the act, hoping that some little boy just like me gets to experience what I did when I got my first bike, is something that for me you can't put a dollar value on. Now that my kids are starting to get old enough to understand the concept of giving without expectation of anything in return I get them involved in choosing the bikes. Hopefully I'll be able to instill in them some of the same principles that my Dad instilled in me and in the future they may carry on the tradition in some fashion.

When I can I also tip big for good service at restaurants, but I always try and slip it into the bill when the waiter isn't looking so they will find it when I've already left, or if that's not possible I'll slip it to them discretely on the way out the door, always making a point to let them know that I thought their service was excellent and that I appreciated how difficult it can be to wait tables. Depending on the type of restaurant and amount of the bill the tip may actually not be that much money in the grand scheme of things, but for that waiter it may represent an hour or two of their work, and it may just make their day. On more than one occasion I have had a waiter or waitress come running out of a restaurant to chase me down in the car park and thank me for a generous tip when they've found it in the bill after I've left. Every time this happens I feel like a million bucks and to experience the joy of the wait staff is the greatest reward.

Likewise, I have a few distinct vivid memories of giving money to people less well off than myself that still make me smile when I think about them. One in particular occurred shortly after the birth of our first son as my wife and I were out to a celebratory dinner with my wife's parents. We had just finished an amazing meal at a new restaurant owned by a celebrity chef when our young son became a bit upset and started crying as babies do. I had taken him out the front of the restaurant to settle him so that his crying didn't disturb other diners, and to allow my wife to catch up with her parents in peace. At the very second I stepped out onto the street a gloss black Lamborghini Gallardo burbled past, the exhaust note from its high-revving V10 engine reverberating magically off the high-rise buildings that lined the street. I'm not sure if that positive experience influenced what I did next or if I would have done it anyway, however as I was rocking my young son back and forth on the footpath to settle him two scraggly looking young men Jaywalked across the road in front of me and as they approached one of them asked me for money for the train. I'm usually not a huge fan of giving money to people who actually ask for it, preferring to donate to the likes of homeless people who are not overtly seeking cash, but for some reason I felt the urge to give this young bloke some cash. I guess I was feeling pretty fortunate having just had an expensive meal at an exclusive restaurant with my beautiful wife, cuddling my perfect first-born son, and having just witnessed my favourite marque of car come by, and I wanted to help the young fellas who clearly hadn't shared the same privileged upbringing that I had. As I got my wallet out the first piece of currency that I saw was a $100 bill and without hesitation I whipped it out and gave it to the young man in front of me. The look of disbelief on his face, and the face of his mate, was priceless. He baulked for a second, looked me in the eye and asked, "are you serious?" and when I confirmed that I was he took the money, literally breaking into a jumping variant of dance celebration and declaring at the top of his voice that I "fucking rocked" before running off down the street with his mate. Now I would be terribly surprised, and a little disappointed, if those two young men *didn't* buy alcohol or drugs with that $100, however the experience of giving it to them was truly joyous. I couldn't tell you what I spent the hundred dollars before or after that on (probably the restaurant bill for the latter!), but the memory of giving that money to those young men is still vivid and still makes me laugh as I write this a decade later. I've come to like thinking of money as described by Jen Sincero in her book titled "You are a badass at making money", as a form of energy that flows to and from you, rather than a scarce resource that must be hoarded.

I've spoken a lot here about the giving of money because I've been lucky enough over the years to have a little spare to give, however the exact same principle and joy applies to the giving of your time, experience, or inexpensive gifts. During my time in the army some of my best memories from deployments were of the reactions from children in third-world countries when given small gifts that a kid from a first-world country would certainly be unimpressed by. I recall many examples of Afghan children being overjoyed by the gift of a ballpoint pen, and one particular instance where I gave a Mars Bar to a young child in regional Afghanistan. The look on his face when that tasty candy hit his taste buds and the sugar hit his system was indescribable! I appreciate that I may have ruined him for life and that he will spend the remainder of his days searching for another Mars Bar fix, but in that moment it was a brilliant experience. Another example occurred in the mountains of East Timor when I gave a young boy a bottle of water. He was overjoyed with what I assumed was having some clean water to drink, however he promptly proceeded to open the bottle, empty the contents right there on the ground at my feet, and then put the lid back on. He simply wanted the container, but nonetheless that experience was also memorable for the joy it created in that little guy's life on the day. Likewise, I've found some of my most medically rewarding moments in helping out those in third-world countries who otherwise wouldn't have had access to any decent form of medical services. Relatively low-level procedures that we take for granted in the first-world can have a massive impact on the life of someone less fortunate. My favourite example to illustrate this point is of a young Afghan boy who had been brought to me by his desperate father in a village in regional Afghanistan. Through an interpreter I was able to ascertain that the young boy had excruciating pain in his right ear and had been unable to sleep or eat for days as a result. In the day prior to me meeting him the young boy had begun to bleed from his ear canal. Despite the language barrier I could see that the father was truly distressed by his son's situation and felt completely helpless to assist him, and as a father myself I felt a deep sense of empathy with the man. After a brief inspection of the ear canal I immediately saw the problem and using a set of tweezers I was able to fairly easily extract the large maggot that had taken up residence in the child's ear canal causing the issue. I was then able to provide pain relief and a course of antibiotics for the child to go on with, and while I wasn't able to follow him up I'm confident that he would have made a full recovery. Even if he didn't (and I truly hope he did!) I had done my very best to help the boy on that day without any expectation of a single thing in return and it felt great. At best he made a full recovery and forever sung the praises of the Australian Army, which is a big part of winning the hearts and minds of a population and defeating an insurgency, or at worst he suffered on with ear issues and needed to seek further review. Like the concept of homeless people buying alcohol with the money you give them, there is little you can do about what happens after your act, but you have full control over the act itself and that's what counts.

In more general terms than RAK specifically, I'm also a big advocate of being generous with your time and experience in whatever field you may have some subject matter expertise in. In my military role this meant investing a lot of time and energy into training those medics that I had the privilege to lead and imparting any knowledge that I had to help them build a skill set that would allow them to do their job on the ground under the worst possible conditions. Admittedly this was part of the role that I was paid to perform but I chose to take it to the next level, more like an obligation to train those medics and share my knowledge with them than a function of my role. Once again, as with the giving of money or gifts to those less fortunate than myself, I felt a great sense of personal satisfaction in helping others achieve competence in a particular skill.

One final point before I bring this chapter to a close, and that is *be kind*! We tell this to our kids all the time but how many of us actually practice what we preach on a day-to-day basis? In my professional role at the time of writing I frequently consult patients who have come from disadvantaged backgrounds, often with issues relating to mental health and drug addiction. The simple act of treating these people with dignity regularly comes as a surprise to them and on many occasions I have had them tell me that they've never been treated that nicely by a doctor in the past. Sadly, they are so used to being treated poorly due to their social disadvantage that they have already judged how I will treat them before our interaction even begins and are surprised when it doesn't play out in the manner that they had imagined. As a society we love to judge others and base our own social worth on our perception of whether we are better or worse than the people around us. Once you take the time to scratch the surface and read past the cover of the book to truly bother to learn why someone is struggling in life you will often find that they have been set on that trajectory from the earliest age through factors that were completely outside of their control. It doesn't cost a single cent to treat these people with human dignity and instead of judging them to make ourselves feel a little more important; we should take every opportunity to see what we might be able to do to help them. You never know when a small gesture as simple and free as human dignity might just make a significant impact on someone's day.

Feed Your Future

I'm an avid reader of motivational books and am fascinated by different author's approaches as to how to become and stay motivated towards moving forward in life. One author I quite enjoy is Grant Cardone, who hit rock bottom in his twenties with drug addiction before recreating himself to be a hugely successful businessman worth hundreds of millions of dollars. For anyone looking into getting one of Grant's books I recommend *Be Obsessed or Be Average* on audio book. Narrated by Grant himself in his irrepressible evangelistic style, he tells his life story with the emphasis on an absolute requirement for obsession in order to be truly successful on a large scale in life. One of the chapters in that book that really struck a chord with me is titled *Feed your Future*.

On listening to Grant's audiobook, it occurred to me that unknowingly somewhere in my early adulthood I fell into the habit of feeding my future. Since the time I entered into medicine and the Army I have always projected forward in my mind what the next step was going to be while I worked on being the best that I could at the stage I was at. I think that for the most part we all feed our future to some degree in our early adulthood out of necessity but for many of us the habit is subconscious and ceases the minute that external forces stop demanding it. Let me explain. Most of us will have gone through school to some level of high school at a minimum. During that time goals are put in front of us, and while they are not necessarily goals of our choosing, they are required nonetheless to pass at school and achieve the grades we need to move onto higher education or training. The goals of school involve a minimum of attendance and passing of exams in our various subjects. These goals are rigid in their criteria and timeframes so we all work toward them in our own way and fumble our way through. If you're anything like me, you will have left your study to the last safe moment and then crammed like mad in the days to weeks before the exam before doing a massive data dump on the day and then forgetting most of the information shortly afterwards. Hopefully some of you reading were a shade more organised than that, however the end result is the same, that being graduation from that phase of your education having potentially fed your future to move onto higher education or trade training. Most of us can't just stop and retire at that point so out of necessity we set a new goal, be it to attend university, trade school, or apply for jobs and enter the workforce. Once again, perhaps not entirely goals of our choosing however at this stage we can take a bit more ownership over our choice which oftentimes leads to a little more engagement in the goal attainment process, and perhaps even a little personal satisfaction in achieving the goals. From there life moves on and new goals come into the picture; harder exams, work promotions, a house, a new car, finding a husband or wife, kids, perhaps post-graduate study, the list goes on. Whether consciously or subconsciously we set goals for ourselves and using a formal approach or otherwise we work out a way to achieve them, all the while feeding our future and continuing to move forward in life. Then something happens to many people as they hit middle age. They've become established in their job and family life, they have the house and car, the kids are in school, and one day starts to merge into the next. They are no longer feeding their future and they get stuck in the rut. They start to realise that perhaps they aren't going to achieve everything that they might have wanted to in life and they aren't getting any younger. They feel like they are treading water and no longer moving forward in life and in a desperate attempt to recapture some of their youth they buy the sports car or motorbike and perhaps even go to the extreme to chase a younger partner to make themselves feel vital again, and the wheels come off life as they know it. We all know this as a midlife crisis, and I suspect many of these cases could be avoided if people had have simply continued to feed their future and move forwards in life in a more gradual and consistent manner. Of those who don't do anything drastic in an attempt to reclaim their youth, most simply stay in their rut and complain about it until the day that they can finally retire. The fact is that it takes effort to initiate change, especially when you're well established and busy in your life, and most people aren't willing to expend the requisite energy to dig themselves out of their rut. This is great news for those who are willing to set goals for positive change because it reduces the competition in whatever field they chose to pursue.

Back in my early twenties when I had finally pulled myself out of my slump of self-pity following my failed professional triathlon aspirations I unknowingly commenced a lifelong habit of feeding my future. By entering into both medical school and the army I took on a new set of significant challenges that once again gave me long-term goals that could be broken down into bite-size pieces that I could chip away at week-in, week-out, building small blocks of accomplishment and self-confidence as I went. To a degree these initial goals were imposed on me by the requirements to pass medical school and the criteria required to commission into the army, and to be honest neither of these aspirations had been long-term ones for me, they were just the best available to me at the time when my previous plans came unglued. That said they were of my own choosing and I could see a future in the end result of becoming an army doctor, so I embraced the challenge. The factor that supercharged my motivation towards not only achieving my goals but also excelling at them was the addition of passion when

I had my eyes opened to Special Forces. All of a sudden I had true purpose in my life and no matter the hardship of study in medical school, working seemingly endless hours as a junior doctor, or the hours of hard physical training for selection, I knew that it all added up to a better chance of reaching my overarching goals. I was truly able to *embrace the suck* because for the first time in my life I had taken complete ownership over my goals. Special Forces was not required of me, it was something that I had chosen to do entirely on my own, and it was therefore something I was willing to sweat, bleed, and sacrifice to achieve. Something that I think is worth noting here I think is the fact that I didn't start down the pathway of military medicine with passion, it developed as I went along. I think most of us believe that unless we feel passion for an outcome before we set the goals to achieve it then they're not the right goals for us. Sometimes out of necessity you need to set the goals first and then either find or potentially create the passion for them as you go along. If you find yourself in the situation where you are in a job or a role that you aren't passionate about, there's never any harm setting goals to excel in that role and see where it takes you. Most likely it will lead you to a better place due to the positive nature of goal setting and attainment and who knows, it may even lead to an opportunity to evolve past your situation and onto something better. If you just stay in the rut you will never know.

Another great saying that fits nicely into this topic

is *comfort is a slow death*. I'm not exactly sure where this one originated from but I became aware of it when I saw it printed on a Tee Shirt from the Australian veteran-owned company Skilled Athlete. I've always found that the times in my life when I'd accomplished my immediate goals and was yet to set new ones have actually been my unhappiest. This sounds completely counterintuitive, as logically it would seem that these periods are when I should have been most content, but I simply wasn't. In these periods I felt stagnant, as though I was wasting time when I could have been using that time to evolve further and start moving towards the next challenge. During those periods I had become comfortable and was starting to slowly die.

As I came to the end of my army Special Forces career I looked ahead at life post-military and it terrified me. The fifteen years of my life leading up to that point had been focused entirely on getting to the position I was at and I was about to step out of that environment and into something completely new. My whole identity at that time was that of a Special Forces doctor and linked to that identity was my self-worth. My entire social support network outside of my immediate family was contained within the army unit I was with and I was about to unplug myself from them and move several states away. I could see that it was going to be a tough time and I predicted that I was headed for a fall. To make matters worse I had accumulated nearly a year of leave that I had never been able to take during my army time due to the operational tempo, putting me in the position of having a lot of time on my hands to sit around and feel sorry for myself if I wasn't careful. I had no real clue what life post-army held for me but the one thing I did know was that I needed to feed my future. Asking around among other unit members who had recently transitioned at the time I learned that several had gone into MBA programs, which piqued my interest. I knew that further study would be a great way to occupy myself during the challenging transition period and an MBA seemed to be a great program to equip myself with a generalised business skill set to transition into the civilian world. I enrolled and was accepted into an online MBA program and I made sure that I maxed out my subject load to give me focus and keep me well and truly busy immediately post-discharge.

As I had predicted, the first couple of years after leaving the army were particularly difficult for me. The significant reduction in tempo of my life coupled with the lack of stimulus in my new life allowed some demons from my army career to finally catch up with me and create problems. When my leave ran out I took a job working fly-in, fly-out as a doctor on a mine site, which only served to compound the situation. In theory the job was outstanding, I was getting paid very well to do very little, but in practice it was terrible. I would sit for hours on end in my clinic, often only seeing a handful of patients a day, and those that I did see where generally for tick-box annual medicals and nothing medically exciting. At night I would return to my tiny portable accommodation room to sleep and do it all again the next day. I was comfortable and I was dying a slow death. I had left the army to spend more time with my family and I found myself away from them almost as much in my new role. On a positive however I had plenty of time to immerse myself in my MBA study, allowing me to really get the most out of the program and expand my mind to business and management principles that I had never had the opportunity to be exposed to prior. As with my medical and military careers prior, I entered into my business studies with no real passion for the area but as I progressed through my MBA that passion grew. Using skills learned through my studies I started a small tactical medical training and consulting company allowing me to reengage in that world that I loved so much through training Police Tactical Groups. This work not only allowed me to recapture some of my previous self-worth, but also provided an additional source of income on my off weeks from the mine site. As my company gained momentum the opportunity came to use the small platform and client base that I had built to negotiate a buy-in to a larger company working in the same field. The company, TacMed Australia, had been founded by and ex-Special Forces medic friend as initially an equipment supply company. TacMed was moving in the direction of providing training at the same time that my company was starting to grow, and it made perfect sense to combine our efforts and form the one company rather than compete head-to-head. This not only allowed me an opportunity to be the part owner of a company which has subsequently grown to have multimillion dollar revenues, but it also allowed me to exercise the theoretical skills that I had learned in my MBA in a practical setting, becoming passionate about the business side of things along the way.

As with my medical and military pursuits prior, I started down the MBA pathway out of a perceived necessity to have something to occupy my mind for the next phase of my life, and with no passion whatsoever for business at the time. Once I got started the passion developed and was then supercharged by the opportunity to train Tactical Police initially, and then later to buy in to TacMed and I've never looked back. It has proven another example of just getting started and letting the rest look after itself. I'm not suggesting that you'll find passion for everything you get started on and it may be that after giving a pursuit a good go you determine that it really isn't for you and the passion never comes. This will happen and it is part of the overall process, there can be no success without the occasional failure. Such a failure occurred to me in the final couple of years of my army career when I first began to see transition to civilian life looming and the need to re-tool for that world. At the time I had initially enrolled in a Masters course in Policing, Intelligence and Counter-Terrorism, thinking that it might be an interesting extension of the work that I had been doing and might open doors into civilian organisations that would allow me to transition out of the military while remaining engaged in a somewhat similar space. I slugged away at the course, staying up late at night to complete the requisite readings and assignments and contorting my other commitments around the required online lectures and group sessions.

During the year that I stuck with that course I took the opportunity to really explore the jobs that it might lead to, I spoke to those doing them and researched the organisations they worked for. After the first year of the course I was certain that it wasn't the direction that I wanted to head in life and I had no passion at all for the study, so I dropped out. While ultimately this can be viewed as quitting or failure, and in a way it was both, I felt that I had given it a good shot and it was clear to me that I was headed down a path that I didn't want to be on. I could have stuck with the course just for the sake of completing it, but it would have been at the expense of the opportunity to study my MBA and open doors to opportunities that I subsequently was able to be passionate about. I think the key point here is that I didn't quit the initial course to sit on the couch and watch Netflix, I quit it to free up capacity in my life to study something different.

The take-home message from this chapter is that you have to continually feed your future and constantly evolve in some aspect of your life. Don't wait for something to come along that you feel passionate about before pursuing it, start the pursuit and wait for the passion to develop. If it doesn't, and you can honestly say to yourself you've given it a good crack, then maybe it wasn't the pursuit for you and you need to change tack and try something new. Just do something! If you feel you need a little motivation to kick-start the process I recommend checking out the book *Crush It* by Gary Vee (Vaynerchuck). If that doesn't get you fired up I don't know that anything will.

Stay Humble but be Certain You Can Achieve Your Goals

Confidence is of course essential in pursuing goals, and if you have no confidence in your ability to achieve a set goal then you are almost certainly destined for failure. Indeed, confidence is implied in the SMART goal process by the very fact that the goal has been considered both Achievable and Realistic, hence you have determined that you are confident the goal can be accomplished. But where does that confidence come from?

It wasn't until I started writing this book that I really gave due consideration to where my confidence to pursue ambitious goals originated from. On reflection I certainly wasn't born with it, as it definitely wasn't there at an early age. Looking back on my primary schooling I was a somewhat shy, chubby kid that due to moving schools every couple of years never really had an established group of friends. I got bullied here and there like many school kids do and as outlined in earlier chapters was profoundly average in my academic and sporting pursuits. On a positive, my regular school moves probably served to build a degree of resilience and out of necessity forced me to develop a set of social skills that allowed me to better integrate into new environments. It wasn't until my final 18 months of high school that I recall having any real self-confidence in any facet of my life, which came through starting to win the odd running race and triathlon. At that stage I lacked confidence in my academic abilities, but my sporting wins served to bolster my overall self-confidence and represented the first examples I can recall of setting and achieving goals in my life. As I progressed on to pursuing triathlon seriously my small progressive gains in my sporting achievements allowed me to continue to gather the confidence to set more and more ambitious goals. At the same time my part-time study of university subjects that actually interested me, and that I could see the practical application for, encouraged me to exercise that muscle leading to building of confidence in the academic realm. As with my sporting confidence, my academic confidence grew over a period of years as ongoing study of subjects that I was passionate about led to better and better marks, which subsequently led to a gradual upward spiral effect of study, results, and confidence. The combination of improvements in my sporting and academic confidence fueled an improvement in my overall self-confidence and resultantly I found myself more outgoing, engaging, and personable than ever before. By the time I finished my first university degree, despite my sporting confidence taking a considerable hit with the realisation that my professional triathlon aspirations were no longer realistic, academically I had built the confidence to step up to the plate and sit the entrance exam for a graduate position in medical school. Medicine was a career that I had never even considered prior to that point in my life, there were no doctors in my family so the job was completely foreign to me, and medical school had been completely inaccessible to me directly out of school due to my mediocre marks. It was only after slowly building academic confidence over a period of years that I was able to muster up the confidence to even attempt the medical school entrance exam. Subsequently getting a high enough mark to apply for medical school further enhanced my academic confidence and coupled with my overall improved self-confidence I was able to successfully interview for both a spot in medical school and the army scholarship scheme to fund my study. Once I got started studying medicine my upward spiral of academic confidence slowly continued as I passed more and more subjects in the course and compounded further as I progressed through subsequent post-graduate specialist medical, and business studies. While the MBA was completely unrelated to my previous field of study, the academic confidence translated across to the new discipline and allowed me to approach the new subject matter confidently.

From a military perspective, the confidence to attempt Special Forces selection came from a combination of confidence gained from my success in selection in both medical school and the military scholarship, backed by the physical confidence that my previous triathlon pursuits gave me to suggest I was up to the challenge. By the time I got to the start line for Special Forces selection there was no doubt in my mind that I could get to the end of the course if I just stayed mentally strong, did my very best, and was lucky enough to remain uninjured. Whether I got selected or not was largely outside of my control, I just had to be there at the end to be in with a chance. As it turned out I did make it to the end of the course and was deemed suitable for further training with the unit, which served to further enhance my military and physical confidence specifically, and more broadly my overall self-confidence.

I think you get the point, my belief is that the confidence to set and achieve highly ambitious life goals is not a characteristic that you either have or haven't been born with, it is one that is gained slowly over years to decades of slow and steady accomplishments that snowball as you go along. I think of confidence like a muscle that you can exercise just like you would exercise your muscles at the gym. Someone with no training couldn't just step up and lift a 150kg deadlift, however if they started with 50kg and then put in appropriate amounts of incremental training over an appropriate amount of time they would likely accomplish the 150kg lift. Furthermore, I strongly believe that the confidence gained in one realm of your life translates to a significant degree into other completely unrelated realms due to its contribution to the enhancement of your overall self-confidence. I managed to go from an average chubby kid with very little confidence to where I am now via a series of incremental and at times imperceptibly small steps over a long period of time, and I believe that everyone is capable of the same progression no matter what age you are at or your starting point.

One key factor that is worthy of discussion here is that while confidence is crucial to goal attainment it is absolutely imperative that the confidence is backed by some degree of tangible evidence to suggest it is warranted. Confidence without a minimum of competence to back it up is false confidence and is almost guaranteed to set you up for failure. False confidence often coexists with arrogance, and even if you have the score on the board to back your confidence, arrogance is a terrible attribute and should be avoided at all costs. I think we can all think of someone arrogant who we have encountered in our lives. Even when these people accomplish the goal that they have often been very loud and obnoxious declaring that they will we still don't like them. And when they fall short of the mark they have set themselves up for a significant fall and much ridicule. Don't be that person; stay humble.

I'd like to share a cautionary tale here of an experience from early in my medical career when my confidence had started to exceed my competence and from which I learned a valuable and lasting life lesson.

The situation occurred when I was a junior doctor and was doing a rotation in a small town in outback Australia. Being one of only two doctors in town at that stage I was afforded the opportunity to practice procedures that I would have been unlikely to have the chance to do in larger centres where more specialist doctors were in abundance. While I was trained in the procedures I was inexperienced, and with hindsight my confidence at the time significantly outweighed my competence making me dangerous. I was conducting a skin lesion excision clinic on the particular day in question and had spent the morning cutting out various moles and other skin lumps and bumps from all manner of patients' body parts. The clinic was going well and as it progressed my false confidence grew and grew right up until the point where it took an abrupt turn for the worse. I had been in the process of removing a cyst from the neck of a middle-aged woman at the time of the event and recall talking jovially with the patient as I did so. The procedure was being performed under local anaesthetic leaving the patient fully conscious and aware, with her neck draped in the usual manner to achieve surgical sterility. I had failed to give due consideration to the underlying anatomy of the woman's neck, most notably the significant series of pipes that carry blood to and from the brain, and as I chatted and chopped my attention was suddenly drawn to a pipeline of a blood vessel pulsating out of the excision site that I was creating by removing the cyst. I immediately froze and stopped talking, the significance of what I had almost done dawning on me at the exact same time as a cold sweat hit my brow and I felt the colour drain from my face. I had in-advertently neatly dissected out the woman's carotid artery and but for the grace of God had not put my scalpel straight through it. I regained my composure and completed the procedure with the woman none the wiser, but myself significantly wiser. To have cut that patient's carotid artery in that remote location would have been an absolute disaster and the very fact that I had almost done it was a direct result of false confidence in my own abilities. As I write this book that event occurred more than 12 years ago, but I still feel my heart race and my palms sweat when I stop to think hard about it. From that day forth I became very cognizant of not allowing my confidence to outweigh my competence, and I never put a knife anywhere near a patient's skin without due consideration of the anatomy below!

Once again the key message of this chapter is to get out there and get started, this time in exercising your confidence muscle. Slowly but surely you will see the gains, just remember not to let your confidence exceed your competence.

Don't Leave Any Rounds in the Magazine

There are lots of motivational sayings relating to not giving up until you quite literally can't go any further, things like *don't leave any gas in the tank* for instance. These relate to the idea that you never quite know when success is right around the corner and just hanging in there for a tiny bit more might get you to your objective. There are sayings for that as well, including; *the night is darkest just before the dawn*, but I like to think of this one in a more military way and use the analogy of not leaving any rounds in the magazine. This one stems from the concept of leaving a bullet or two in your magazine in the combat environment in order to give you the option to turn the rifle on yourself as an alternative to falling into enemy hands if all had gone to custard and it looked as though you may be about to get captured. It is the stuff that gets glamourised in war movies for the most part, but something that I actually found myself pondering seriously prior to my first tour of Afghanistan. It was assumed that any coalition soldier falling into enemy hands in that theatre was in for a particularly rough time, and the thought of a swift ending at your own hand might have been a fairly reasonable alternative. I dismissed the idea outright myself for a couple of reasons. First of all, I was always pretty rubbish at counting the number of rounds that I had shot, especially under the heightened state associated with a tactical situation, and I figured that I would be little to no chance of pulling up with one or two rounds left in my final magazine if it came to that. Secondly, you just never know how things are going to play out. It would be a terrible shame to turn the rifle on yourself only to have a helicopter gunship show up overhead a few seconds later or a support element arrive to save you only to find you with a rifle in your mouth! In my opinion I might as well keep shooting until my rifle went click instead of bang, and then cross that bridge when I got there. I had a lot to live for and I was resigned to staying alive at all costs and seeing how the chips might fall in the worst-case scenario. Many years later I had the chance to hear a first-hand account of a British SAS soldier from the ill-fated and much publicised *Bravo Two Zero* patrol in the first Gulf War, who had been captured and tortured by Iraqi forces and then subsequently released. While his vivid recollections of the torture he endured were chilling to say the least, to his credit he had managed to physically and psychologically move past the ordeal and return back to his role as an SAS soldier. Hearing his remarkable story solidified my stance for future deployments that I would leave no rounds in the magazine if it came to it and see how it all played out. Thankfully it was a decision I never had to make for real.

Translating that analogy into a far less dramatic metaphoric application I had an experience on my Special Forces selection course where my overwhelming desire was to quit but, largely thanks to the motivation provided by another candidate, I managed to push on and fire the last few rounds in my magazine. The event occurred on a section of the course involving a five-day individual navigation exercise comprising long distance hikes in a national park between check points at the tops of mountains while carrying a very heavy pack. The real challenge of the exercise was a psychological one in that we were provided no indication as to how much distance we needed to cover or how many checkpoints we needed to reach to pass the activity. We were left completely to our own devices and needed to pace ourselves to cover as much or as little ground as we felt reasonable, all the while keeping in mind the fact that there was a further five days of the selection course to go afterwards. We were under strict instructions not to interact with other candidates during the activity and for the most part the individual routes between checkpoints that we had all been allocated meant that full days could pass without seeing other candidates anyway. I had crossed paths with a few others over the first couple of days and we had played by the rules and given one another nothing more than a nod of acknowledgement before proceeding on our separate ways. On the morning of the final day of the activity I bumped into another candidate in a deep creek line I was moving along and figuring that the chance of getting caught was slim, took the chance to have a quick chat. The topic of that discussion centred on how much distance we had both covered and how many checkpoints we had hit. During the conversation the other candidate told me with a decent degree of conviction that a minimum of five checkpoints were required to pass the activity, and without really questioning the authenticity of his information I took it as gospel. We wrapped up our conversation and parted ways leaving me to ponder my situation. I had hit four checkpoints by that point and my fifth was at the very top of a mountain some 20km away. We were under instruction not to move after dark which left me with about seven hours to get to it. By that stage we were a couple of weeks into the selection course and my body was starting to show some wear and tear. I had strained one of my quadriceps muscles quite badly and it was giving me hell with every step, and I had started to lose a considerable amount of weight from the intense physical exertion of the course and the limited food provided. My physical deterioration was starting to take a toll on my psychological state and for the first time on the course I was having moments of mental weakness and doubt. I trudged along throughout the rest of the final day of the activity and was approaching the base of the mountain that my fifth checkpoint sat atop of as the sun started to get low on the horizon. By that time I had resigned myself to the fact that I wouldn't make it to the checkpoint before dark and I had decided to set up camp at the base of the mountain for the night and radio in my location for the scheduled pick up the following morning. In the final few hundred metres of stomping towards the base of the mountain another candidate came charging up from behind without me noticing and drew level with me, scaring the life out of me as he did so. It turned out that his next checkpoint was the same one as mine, but unlike me his attitude was positive and despite acknowledging that he wasn't going to make the checkpoint before dark he was going for it anyway. He urged me to do the climb with him, but I was mentally defeated at the time and when we hit the start of the track leading up the mountain I wished him the best of luck and then found a place to camp for the night and dropped my pack. Although I had made my decision to quit something inside of me didn't allow me to unpack my kit to set up camp. As I sat there dejected I turned my gaze to the other candidate in the distance making his way up the climb to the checkpoint as the sun began to set. I ran all the years of training that had led up to that point through my mind and as I did so it occurred to me that they had all led to that moment and I was in the very process of giving up on my dream. I had the sickening realisation that everything that I had worked so hard for, and all the sacrifices I had made may have been all for nothing if I didn't at least give that final climb a crack. My fifth checkpoint was less than a kilometre away, albeit all uphill, and I wouldn't get there before dark, but I'd rather take a beasting from an angry SAS soldier at the checkpoint for moving after dark than live the rest of my days knowing that I'd let myself down by quitting on my dream. I slung my pack back onto my aching shoulders and with my lungs and legs burning I made the best pace I was capable of up the mountain track as the light faded. As it got darker and darker I got more and more frantic, stumbling on the rocky track underfoot as I raced toward the summit, the close foliage surrounding the track grabbing at my shoulders and pack as I ploughed on. By the time the tracked levelled out and I neared the checkpoint I was in a trance-like state, fueled by the endorphins that my body was spewing out in response to the extreme exertion of the climb and the pain from my strained quadriceps muscle. I paused for an instant to catch my breath and focused my eyes through the darkness to see the faint glow of a light at the checkpoint. With absolutely nothing left to lose I made my way to the checkpoint and, bracing for the worst, announced myself to the Directional Staff there. Without any emotion whatsoever, he proceeded to radio in to the higher command that I had reached the checkpoint and then he promptly dismissed me, instructing me to set up camp nearby and to make my way back down to the base of the mountain in the morning for pickup.

Rudyard Kipling captures the essence of this experience for me eloquently in his poem "If" with the following line:

If you can force your heart and nerve and sinew to serve your turn long after they are gone, and so hold on when there is nothing in you except the Will which says to them "Hold on!"

I truly believe that I reached the very state that Kipling was referring to on that evening on selection. To this day I have no idea as to whether reaching that fifth checkpoint was important or not, it may have been that I had done enough to pass the activity by the time I got to the base of the climb and I could have just camped there and still been allowed to progress on the course. Regardless, I have forever since been glad that I made the decision to tackle that climb as even if it had no bearing on my being allowed to continue and subsequently successfully pass the course, it represented a mental turning point for me on selection. From that point onward, I was unwavering in my resolve to finish the course and no matter how tough it got I never even allowed another thought of self-doubt to enter my mind. I had smashed through a barrier of exhaustion and physical pain, and in doing so had proven to myself what was possible if I could just keep my mind in the game. I had fired every last round in my magazine on that night and the following morning I was still there and still putting one foot in front of the other, every second edging closer to my objective.

Of course, there is a limit to how far any human can push themselves both physically and psychologically, and I was lucky not to succumb to my physical injuries or infection on my selection course. Had that happened I believe that I would have eventually come to terms with the fact that those outcomes were largely outside of my control, and with time have come to accept them. Had I have not gotten up on that evening and attempted that final climb and then subsequently been removed from the course due to a failure to reach the fifth checkpoint I am certain that I would have regretted my decision for the remainder of my days, as that decision was well and truly within my power to influence.

The point of this chapter is this: if you have a life goal that you are set on achieving, don't leave a single round in your magazine in your effort to achieve it. You just never know when that final effort towards your objective might be the difference between success and failure.

Give and Take Second Chances but Think Carefully about Third

When I was 16 years old I was given a second chance that with hindsight changed the course of my life. I was in grade 11 at the sixth school that I had attended over the course of my life to that point and I absolutely hated it. My parents, God bless them, had enrolled my brother and I into the best private school in the town we were living and on reflection must have been making significant financial sacrifices to pay the fees to keep us there. It was a traditional Old English style all-boys school that had a strong culture of rugby and academics and was full of clean-cut, grain-fed country boys who fit the mould. I on the other hand was more interested in growing my hair a little longer and my main passion at the time was art, more specifically aerosol art or graffiti. As the reader will appreciate those two cultures were somewhat incompatible and resultantly my time at that school was thoroughly unenjoyable. I fell in with the wrong crowd and started doing all the usual things that a 16-year-old in the wrong crowd does. I began skipping school, and when I was there I was disengaged and uninterested. My marks suffered and after a few run-ins for various misdemeanors everything came to a head midway through grade 11 with my expulsion. Although I didn't appreciate it at the time it was a crucial period in my life and my poor parents were at their wits' end as to what to do with me. Convinced that I would be happier at an alternative private school on the other side of town I talked my parents into putting in an application to enroll me there. Naturally there was an interview process involved, which I had anticipated to be more of an interrogation than an interview based on my expulsion from the former school. On my very best behavior I attended the interview with the headmaster of the new school, and to my pleasant surprise was met not by an interrogator but by a compassionate gentleman who judged me for the person who I was rather than what I had done, and who appeared to have a genuine interest in my art. I immediately warmed to the headmaster and by the end of the interview I was determined not to get in trouble at his school out of respect to the fact that he had been so welcoming. In fact, the only reference that was made at all to my expulsion from my previous school was a comment accompanied by a smile of "I'm sure we won't have any further issues like that here", and that was that. I had a fantastic time at that new school and ended up fitting in perfectly, excelling in their art program, and winning the school cross-country in my two final years of high school. The second chance that I had been provided proved pivotal to my senior schooling and not only stopped me from progressing down the negative pathway I was on but started to build my self-esteem and sense of accomplishment and confidence that came from my achievements. My graduating marks weren't great by any means; however they were enough to get a start at university, which allowed me to subsequently go on to eventually complete my medical degree. I was well into my early twenties by the time it truly registered what a profound impact that second chance had on my life, and sadly by the time I thought to seek out the headmaster to thank him I learned that he had passed away from cancer. While I unfortunately didn't get the chance to shake that headmaster's hand and thank him for the second chance he had provided me, I would always think of his compassion when I had the opportunity to provide second chances throughout my subsequent careers.

During my time as a Special Forces doctor I had the privilege of leading the medical elements of the units I was attached to and in that role I was accountable for the standard of their performance. I took that responsibility extremely seriously, interpreting any failure of one of the medics under my command as a failure in my leadership and provision of training. Owing to the fact that those medics would frequently find themselves forward deployed with Special Forces elements conducting combat operations, a failure on their behalf could quite literally result in the preventable death of one of our team, which was of course a completely unacceptable outcome. As such I held my medics to a high standard but always made sure that I held myself to a higher standard. For the most part the medics under my command rose to the standard set and on countless occasions excelled when called upon to treat wounded teammates in dire situations. Invariably however there was the occasional medic who would find their way into one of the elements I commanded who clearly didn't meet the requisite standard set for the job. In those instances, I would always make the time to retrain that medic and provide the opportunity for them to work hard to prove themselves worthy of the role, however if they still fell short of the mark I would swiftly do everything within my power to have them removed from the unit. As harsh as this sounds Special Forces will never be an equal opportunity employer and while I could squeeze in the time for second chances, the tempo of the organisation left no capacity for third and fourth chances. Furthermore, the decision to remove underperforming medics from their roles was as protective for them as it was for the soldiers that they would potentially be treating. I know of several medics, military and civilian alike, who have found themselves in medical situations that they felt completely incompetent to control and subsequently resulted in loss of life. The psychological impact on those medics knowing that they didn't have the skillset required to save potentially salvageable casualties has been understandably psychologically debilitating.

What I came to find on several occasions with medics who had failed to meet the mark even after retraining, and whom I was seeking to dismiss, was that their previous performance reports had always been glowing. What this created was a history of excellent work performance on paper contrasting with one bad report from myself, which quite rightly didn't equate to grounds for removal from their role. Upon scratching the surface in these situations it universally turned out that the medics had been under-performing in prior postings however previous bosses had not had the tough conversation with the medic to let them know their deficits and to mark them down on their performance appraisals. It was easier not to rock the boat, not to have the uncomfortable confrontation, and simply wait out the medic's time at their unit and then let them post out to be someone else's problem. As problematic as it was to inherit such a medic into a high-tempo unit, it was also profoundly unfair on the medic themselves, as without having been made aware of their deficiencies they had been denied any opportunity to improve on them and become competent. I always made a point of being very firm but very fair with those under my command and left no ambiguity as to where they stood compared to the standard I expected. I was quick to praise when medics excelled but by the same token I made no effort to sugarcoat a sub-standard performance. In my opinion everyone deserved a second chance, but rarely a third. If anyone reading this book is in a position of leadership with a responsibility to assess the performance of those under you in the command structure I would implore you to have the tough conversa-tions with them and record those conversations formally.

Not only will this create the reporting trail required to have them retrained or ultimately removed should they continue to underperform, but it will make the employee aware of their deficits and give them the opportunity to improve on them if they choose to. In my experience some of the very best medics I had the privilege of working alongside were the very same ones that I had ripped strips off for substandard performances along the way. While it was always uncomfortable to do, and they didn't thank me at the time, several of them made the point of getting in touch with me years down the track and thanking me for yelling at them! Naturally the civilian world with its rigid Human Resource policies is a very different beast to Army Special Forces and a slightly more emotionally intelligent approach is required to counsel employees, however the principles remain the same; give second chances, confront and address underperformance, move to dismiss when all else fails, and don't post your problem.

Several years after transitioning out of the army I found myself in another situation where I was in need of a helping hand, and as with my high school experience with the headmaster, I was afforded a life-changing opportunity by another brilliant human being. At that stage I had found myself struggling to find my new identity as a civilian doctor and professionally under-stimulated by my fly-in, fly-out work role at a mine site. A few demons from my military time were catching up with me and my life was once again headed in the wrong direction. Knowing that

I couldn't bear to stay in the job at the mine site long-term I started looking around for other jobs and in doing so got in touch with a fellow ex-army doctor colleague to provide a reference for me. The doctor in question had previously completed an MBA and was at the time the Medical Superintendent at a small regional Australian hospital. As fate would have it his Deputy Medical Superintendent had recently had to resign for family reasons leaving a vacancy in the role. Despite only being half way through my MBA at the time I was offered the Deputy role, and within weeks of that initial offer both my wife and myself resigned from our jobs at the time, we pulled the kids out of school mid-year, and moved half way across the country for me to take up the new position and start our new lives. While my CV met the minimum standard for the new role I was acutely aware that there would have been much more qualified applicants out there, and that the fact I had served both domestically and in the deployed military setting with the Medical Superintendent was the primary reason that I was offered the opportunity. I knew that he was offering me a helping hand to get my get my career and life back on track and as such I was determined to do everything within my capability to not let him down.

For the two and a half years following I worked 10-13 hour shifts six days out of every ten, never took a single sick day, and pulled extra shifts when other doctors did. It was fantastic. The learning curve was tremendous, requiring me to relearn a bunch of old medical skills that I hadn't required in my military role, as well as new skills relating to both my medical and management role. For the first time since leaving the army I felt a sense of self-worth and accomplishment returning, I finally had purpose back in my professional life and felt as though I was evolving and moving forward. Of course, I made mistakes as I went along and when I did the Medical Superintendent would sit me down and hit me straight between the eyes with what I had done wrong, the implications, and how I could do better next time, before shaking my hand and sending me back to work. Firm but fair, exactly as I had treated those under my leadership in the army.

My contract at the regional hospital was always going to be finite, with the intention of moving back to my wife's hometown at its conclusion to get the kids established in schools before they got much older and the move would be more disruptive to them. As I entered the last year of my contract I started putting out feelers for jobs that might suit me after we moved back. With about nine months left on my contract I saw a job advertised as the Medical Director for a statewide capability that I thought would be perfect for me. It looked interesting, was in the town we were moving back to, and required the very combination of medical and management qualifications that by that stage I had. The only problem was they wanted someone to start immediately leaving me with the dilemma of not wanting to let down the very person who had provided me the opportunity for the role I was in, versus the potential to land the perfect job for the next phase of my life. After seeking out more information about the advertised job and deliberating for a couple of days I decided the best approach was to have a chat with the Medical Superintendent about the situation and get his opinion. As with my experience with the headmaster all those years prior, the Medical Superintendent not only understood my desire to apply for the new role but more or less insisted that I did. He could see that it was an outstanding opportunity for me professionally and despite the fact that it would leave his capability with a significant position to fill he was completely supportive of my application, providing a glowing reference. I managed to negotiate a solution whereby I stayed on in my role at the time for a few more months while they held the new job for me, and then I moved to start the new job leaving my wife and kids behind for several months to finish out the school year. The logistics of the whole situation were clunky, and it would have been easier not to do it and just stay in my old job until I had finished my contract and then take whatever job was going at the time in the new location. My assessment however was that the new job was too good to pass up and would be worth the hassle required to facilitate the transition. The fact that the Medical Superintendent was so supportive of the situation was just a refreshing bonus and another fantastic example to me of the difference that emotionally intelligent and genuinely kind people in positions of authority can make.

There are several points that I wanted to convey in

this chapter, the first of which being the giving of second chances and helping hands to those in need. Without being afforded the opportunities described above I'm certain that my life would have taken a very different trajectory. On the flipside of the second chances and helping hands, don't be too proud to accept one if it's offered to you and you are in need, however if you do take it make sure that you work your fingers to the bone to honour the opportunity and validate the decision that was made by the person providing it. The final point is that if you find yourself stuck in a rut look far and wide for a solution to get yourself out of it. In the example provided in this chapter my family and I moved several states away in the middle of the school year to take the opportunity provided and then several states back at the end of it. I appreciate that my nomadic lifestyle throughout my youth and military career made the barriers to this move much lower than for many people but nonetheless it was still a significant decision to make with a family. If you've weighed up your situation and your assessment is that a move across the country or across the world may be the legitimate solution, then don't exclude it without adequate consideration it just might be the answer.

Stop Moving the Goddamn Goal Posts!

There's a great line out of Max Ehrmann's 1927 poem *Desiderata* that is relevant to this chapter and reads:

Enjoy your achievements as well as your plans.

Much of what I have written about to this point relates to always setting more and more ambitious goals, with the implication being that there is never really a point where you can be satisfied with what you've achieved and finally rest on your laurels. While I do believe in the importance of continually moving forward in life and challenging ourselves, I've also come to realise that it is equally as important to enjoy your accomplishments and reflect periodically on how far you've come. The key is to strike a balance between striving towards a life goal and hitting it, taking some time to enjoy the achievement, but then setting another goal before you have the chance to get comfortable and start to stagnate.

Failure to enjoy your achievements and acknowledge

your progress can lead to a degree of burn out, which I experienced myself towards the end of my time as a doctor with Special Forces. By that stage I had spent five years in fundamentally the same role, including four operational tours of Afghanistan. It was a fast-paced job and at a time when the world of military tactical medicine was evolving rapidly with new technologies offering enhanced survivability to critically injured casualties on the battlefield. The US were leading the charge in capability development and with close ties to the US Special Operations medical community we had almost immediate access to any new kit that they had developed. The issue came with getting Australian authorisation to use it on our soldiers, as a lot of the new technologies hadn't been extensively tested to develop the evidence-base to confirm beyond doubt that they worked and were safe. The way I viewed it we were playing a high-stakes game where our guys were periodically dying on the battlefield before they could be evacuated to higher medical care, and in my opinion we had absolutely nothing to lose by trying even the most experimental of techniques at the point of injury to try and save them. I was caught up in the bubble that surrounded Special Forces and what we did, and I was so completely fixated on the capability that we *didn't* have that I'd lost sight of just how far we had come. I was hung up on getting from 98% to 100% and was spinning my wheels writing briefs and pressuring the military medical hierarchy for the extra 2% that I thought might just give us an outside chance of making a life or death difference.

With hindsight I can see that from the perspective of the military medical hierarchy there was absolutely no justification to approve what I was requesting and that they were already accepting significant risk by allowing us to operate at the level that we were at the time, which was significantly higher in some areas than our regular army counterparts. I also found myself becoming more and more frustrated with the hierarchy within my own unit, who I perceived were underutilising the capability that I felt my medical element could offer, once again losing sight of the fact that we were being well integrated into operations and only occasionally being left off jobs due to strategic priorities or space limitations on insertion platforms.

I was falling into the trap of what the unit referred to as *creeping excellence*, in effect the continual moving of the goal posts further and further away with the ultimate result of never actually being able to kick a goal. Rather than acknowledging the achievement of any of the goals I had set I was continually stretching the initial goal or merging it with others in an attempt to achieve more. While there is a school of thought that this can be a good thing as it keeps you motivated and striving forward, I found that after five years of chasing goal posts without actually ever taking the time to enjoy the significant achievements that our element had made, that I became jaded and burned out. Indeed, this very psychological stress of ever moving goal posts is used to great effect in Special Forces selection courses where a task will be set, for instance to pack-march to a certain destination in time to get on a truck that will take you home. As the candidates approach the truck it will kick over and drive a further distance away before parking again, prompting another mad scramble to get to it in time, and so on and so forth. Ultimately this kind of psychological stress breaks many candidates and causes them to quit and withdraw from the course. The exact same psychological stress is at play if you fall into the creeping excellence trap and don't allow yourself the occasional satisfaction of achieving your goals and enjoying it.

By the time I left Special Forces I was quite bitter and resentful of the organisation and it took me years of reflection to see the situation in a different light. I realise now with hindsight that we were actually doing some amazing work, and the efforts of those I had the privilege of commanding compounded by the capability that we were afforded unquestionably resulted in the saving of lives that would have otherwise been lost on the battlefield. I couldn't see this at the time owing to the fact that I was fixated solely on the capability we didn't have and the lives we couldn't save. I can also now see that the commanders who I had perceived as ignorant for not embracing my medical plans more entirely would actually have been balancing them carefully against the need to project as much firepower forward as possible to ensure mission success and couldn't compromise this on account of having half a helicopter full of medics just in case of casualties. I have no regrets about my mentality when I was in the job and make no apologies for my behavior, as I wouldn't have felt I was doing my absolute best any other way and I honestly believe that my constant striving led to a degree of enhancement of our overall capability. Ultimately the failure to ever allow myself to enjoy any of the achievements I was involved in led me to the negative state of mind I was in at the end of my Special Forces career and took me years reflect more positively on.

The first time I actually felt like I truly allowed myself to enjoy the achievements of my army career came several years after I had left Special Forces. The Australian Army School of Heath was putting together a *Wall of Valour* for all of the Medical Corps personnel who had been recognised for gallantry and bravery during the Afghanistan campaign. I happened to be among the dozen or so medicos who had been awarded such an honour and as such was invited to the unveiling of the wall, which was made up of photos, medal replicas, and the brief citations of the events associated with our individual awards. My initial inclination was to decline the invite, suspecting that the ceremony would be embarrassing and awkward, however after chatting with a few of my other mates who were also invited we decided as a group to attend. I'm truly glad that I did and although my time out in front of the crowd as my citation was read was exactly as embarrassing and awkward as I had predicted, to be present as all the other citations were read and to see the pride in the face of the other recipients and the genuine appreciation from the audience for the cumulative effort of the recipients filled me with pride and allowed me for the first time to finally acknowledge that I had hit many of my military goals after all. Had I have allowed myself to enjoy the occasional achievement during my military career perhaps I wouldn't have reached the same state of resentment and burn-out that I did, who knows? Perhaps I would have rested on my laurels and not continued to push the capability forward. No one can say for sure, but what I can say with certainty now is that when I set a goal I leave the goalposts exactly where they are and then enjoy kicking the goal for a while before I set a new set of goal posts somewhere in the distance.

Recalibrating the Suck Meter – the Tale of Devaluing Two Supercars

During one of my tours of Afghanistan, I can't remember exactly which one; I was given a small novelty Velcro patch that had an image of a gauge on it. The gauge was divided into three equal sections, green to the left, orange in the middle, and red on the right. Underneath the gauge were the words *Suck Meter* and the dial of the gauge was pointed firmly in the red, indicating that the Suck Meter was maxed out. When I got the patch it was nothing more than a moderately amusing token that seemed somewhat appropriate to the environment in Afghanistan at the time. I have subsequently come to think of the patch as perfect a way of helping the uninitiated to understand a concept known as Post-Traumatic Growth (PTG) which is the lesser known cousin of Post-Traumatic Stress Disorder (PTSD). You see there are people among us who experience extreme trauma, suffer post-traumatic stress (PTS), and then instead of suffering from the sustained negative emotional sequela that defines PTSD, they actually rise up from the low point in their life to be a stronger and more appreciative person then they were prior to the traumatic events. I know this because I am one of them. You see most of us float along in our middle class first-world existence and our Suck Meter is calibrated against our day to day experiences. This is very normal and natural, as we simply don't have any other basis for comparison to allow otherwise. This calibration has our day-to-day activities where we have a roof over our heads, plenty of food to eat, school or a job to go to, running water, flushing toilets etc. as orange on the Suck Meter. This is our norm, it is unexceptional, and it is neither good nor bad, just orange. To tip the needle into the green we need an experience in excess of our norm, which may come in the form of a small win of money on the horse races, a date with a good-looking guy or girl that we're interested in, a promotion at work, a new car or something of the like. Conversely, to tip the dial into the red we need to deviate in a negative fashion from the norm, which might be something as simple as the hot water system failing or a speeding fine. Because we are calibrated to a comfortable middle-class existence these rather trivial events in the grand scheme of things actually ruin our day, if not our whole week. Eventually we get over them and the Suck Meter needle moves from the red back into the orange when the hot water comes back on or when we've paid our fine and moved on with our lives.

I can remember the exact day that my Suck Meter began

recalibrating, although I didn't realise it at the time, it was in Afghanistan on a very specific day in May 2011. The painful recalibration process began with an earthshaking explosion that erupted from an enemy compound approximately 150 metres directly to my front, in which we knew one of our elements had been conducting an assault to neutralise a series of enemy machinegun positions. The explosion occurred about 36 hours into what had been near non-stop combat since we had inserted and fought our way into the enemy stronghold, and the ferocity of the blast caused everyone to stop shooting and turn their attention to the plume of smoke and dust rising from the site of the explosion. For an eerie twenty-odd seconds everything fell silent before the village erupted in gunfire again and our radios began buzzing with casualty reports and commands to coordinate a response. I joined a Quick Reaction Force (QRF) and within minutes we negotiated our way forward through the complex series of mud-brick compounds and alleyways to the incident site. What met our QRF was a scene that would be replayed on loop in my mind for years to follow and would redefine what the red zone of my personal Suck Meter actually looked like. As I knelt in the bloodstained Afghan dirt over the horribly damaged body of my dying friend and desperately tried to save his life, enemy bullets snapping overhead and my teammates returning fire as I did so, my recalibration unknowingly began. Ultimately, I would be beaten by the severity of my friend's injuries on the day and I would be forced to make the impossibly difficult decision to cease our futile resuscitative efforts and turn our attention to the other casualties from the incident, as well as the deteriorating tactical situation. In the following six weeks I would find myself in another two similar situations with the same outcome, two further dead teammates.

Upon return from that tour of Afghanistan I was wound tight with symptoms of Post-Traumatic Stress and had no real idea what to do with myself. I felt out of place back in my comfortable Australian middle-class life, and was struggling to reintegrate with my family unit. I was racked with guilt over the outcome of the deaths of my teammates and was also experiencing a significant degree of survivor guilt. I was hypervigilant, highly anxious in public places, was experiencing intrusive flashbacks and struggling to sleep. I had returned to Australia just prior to the Christmas period and had a six-week block of leave on my return, further isolating me from the social support of being with my teammates from work who had shared my experiences. It was horrible. My solution to the problem was what any caveman would do in this situation – to retreat into my cave. In this instance that meant deciding that my classic red Lamborghini desperately needed to be gloss black, and that I would take my six-week Christmas holiday period to repaint it myself. Much to my wife's delight (as you can imagine!) I disappeared into the garage for 10-12 hours a day and stripped every panel of my car down, sanding back the existing paintwork and priming panels inside and out for a complete colour change. I had re-sprayed a few cars prior to that with a moderate degree of success and was confident that I could do justice to the Italian classic. During the period of the re-spray I was distant from my wife and kids and with hindsight what I was actually doing was a process of decompression, using the isolation of my garage time to try and organise my experiences in my mind and attempt to make sense of them. My wife, God bless her once again, gave me this space and was there for me when I needed her but never once hassled me about my incredibly selfish and unusual way to spend my post-deployment leave period. As time went by and the job progressed things were looking surprisingly good on the car. Nearing the end of the six-week period the initial coats of gloss black were going on nicely and looked menacingly mean on the low-slung sportscar. At the last safe moment and against my initial plans for the re-spray I decided that a few coats of clear on top of the black paint would really give depth to the colour. It was at this point, nearing the end of six weeks of 10 to 12-hour days stripping, sanding, priming and painting, as I laid on the clear paint that I completely ruined the paintjob. For reasons that to this day I can't understand the clear coats reacted with the underlying black paint and caused the paintwork on the entirety of the car to slowly begin to blister and bubble. As you can imagine I was absolutely furious! What I had seen as a satisfying project to work on while I decompressed from a stressful tour, had led to a disastrous outcome that had actually devalued my car. I had spent my entire period of leave in the garage and the result was a car that looked significantly worse than when I started with it, and it was then time to go back to work. Taking a step back from that situation, because of my psychological state at that period of my life I had lost perspective on the fact that I was lucky enough to own one of 500 or so of that model of Lamborghini ever made, and I was beside myself with fury because I had botched the paintwork on it. I imagine that most people reading this can associate with my feelings at the time, because most readers will have a Suck Meter calibrated for middle class first-world life, where these things seem to matter. With hindsight I can thankfully now laugh about that situation, and my Lamborghini still wears the same shitty coat of paint that I put on it all those years ago, which has unsurprisingly not gotten any better with age!

Over the ensuing years I would struggle with periods of PTS, and would return to Afghanistan multiple further times, further filling my bucket of trauma with experiences of death and disfigurement of both soldiers I knew and innocent local-national bystanders, including women and children who got caught up in the conflict. Throughout all of this I was lucky to never get significantly physically injured myself, and to have the loving support network of a very patient wife and close family members. As I transitioned out of the army and moved on with civilian life I rode the rollercoaster of highs and lows that went with that transition. Slowly but surely however as time from my experiences passed I emerged out of the other side of my Post-Traumatic Stress, initially to a point where the dreams disappeared and the intrusive thoughts, while still present, didn't cause my palms to sweat or my heart to race. From there an unexpected thing happened. As further time passed I found that not only were the dreams gone and the intrusive thoughts becoming less frequent, but also I began to see the world around me in a very different light. I would find myself marveling in the mundane. Having seen the horrendous rotting meat and produce at the regional markets of a third-world warzone I would find myself in awe of the abundance of fresh choices available at my local supermarket. Having seen kids ripped limb from limb by explosive devices gave me a newfound appreciation for my own kids, and the simple pleasure of being able to safely play at a local park without the fear of their every step being their last. Having watched my friends and teammates die on the battlefield I felt a new obligation to really live my life to honour them. I spent more time with my kids because my friends were robbed of the same opportunity with theirs; I invested more in my relationship with my wife for the same reason. The devastation that I saw on the faces of the parents of my dead friends at their funeral services caused me to further invest in my relationship with my own parents. I began to see the minutia of life for exactly what it was. I had taken a very large step back and for the first time I was able to see the forest in its amazing entirety as opposed to fixating on the individual trees.

What had happened slowly but surely was a recalibration of my Suck Meter that saw my red zone significantly redefined and that allowed my day-to-day life to now be firmly in the green zone, as opposed to the orange. Simple negative events that were fundamentally inconsequential were seen as exactly that, and no longer affected me like they previously had. Even more significant negative life events would only bump me down to the orange zone at worst, and only for very brief periods of time.

Fast-forward to 2018 and I had another example of devaluing a classic Italian thoroughbred to compare my botched Lamborghini paintjob to. This time it was one of Maranello's finest, a low-mileage 1983 Ferrari that I had acquired with the intention of putting in storage for investment purposes. After searching far and wide I came across the perfect car for my purposes. It had less than 27,000 miles on the clock, was completely unmolested, its original paintwork was in great condition, and its bodywork was straight as an arrow. After over a month of logistics to purchase the car, organise storage, and have it trucked from interstate, it finally arrived! I was about excited as a bloke could get when the car carrier turned up with the gleaming prancing horse strapped to the tray. That excitement grew to fever pitch when I heard the car's high revving engine fire up for the first time as the delivery guy backed it off the car carrier. A couple of signatures later and it was all mine, although as the car was unregistered the extent of my driving of it would be a quick lap around the storage facility and then into the garage I had rented. Now, for anyone who has had a wander around a storage facility they will know that the driveways are narrow and the units are packed in with the obvious objective of maximising the number of units on the premises. This led to a challenging scenario when it came to attempt to shoehorn the rather wide Italian thoroughbred into my storage unit. Further increasing the challenge of the process was a slight slope up into the unit and limited rear vision out of the car. After performing a 15-point turn to align the car as best I could to the unit entrance I began to edge backwards into the garage, riding the clutch as I did so, and frantically alternating my gaze between the two side mirrors to monitor my progress. I heard the sound of the side of the car scraping against the rail of the garage door just moments before I felt the jolt and vibration of the damage being done to the passenger's side. It turns out that what I could see in the wing mirror and the widest part of the side of the car were two different things, and I had gone and gouged a big chunk out of the side of the Italian classic. The very car that had remained as straight as an arrow throughout its 35 years of life ended up getting significantly devalued within about 15 minutes of me owning it. To make matters worse, as the car was going into storage and never intended for road use, the insurance that I had taken out on it did not cover the damage. I was pissed, however in stark contrast to the Lamborghini paintwork incident all those years before which had left me in the red zone for months, the Ferrari incident had relatively minimal impact. Don't get me wrong, I spent a day or two in the orange zone, but I was able to put perspective on it. Ultimately if the worst thing to happen in my week was that I'd scratched the side of my classic Ferrari which I was putting in storage due to my home garage being occupied by my classic Lamborghini (with a shitty paintjob) then life probably wasn't really that bad now was it? I know that this is an extreme example, and I'm privileged to be the custodian of such cars, but I'm sure the reader can get the point of the story. I can maintain perspective now on what is important in life and what isn't due to experiencing a recalibration of my Suck Meter through my military service experiences. Others manage to do it through recovery from all different manner of bad experiences, and then there are those enlightened ones who manage to achieve this perspective without a negative experience to bounce back from. This is the gold standard, and if you've achieved it I take my hat off to you! For everyone else – I wouldn't wish the trauma required to experience Post-Traumatic Growth on any of you, but if you can manage to take a step back and look at your life for what it is and get the perspective to edge that Suck Meter more towards the green than the orange more regularly, the world all of a sudden becomes a fairly magical place to be.

Leadership, Accolades, and Money

Over the course of my military and medical careers to date I've had the opportunity to lead, and be led by, all caliber of men and women, some very impressive and others not so much. While the circumstances of individual interactions differed significantly throughout my time I have identified some common themes that I believe separate good leaders from bad. I believe the most profound attribute that affects leadership ability is whether the individual is most concerned with the opinion of those above them in the chain of command or those below. Universally the best leaders that I have encountered were those whose focus was on the men and women under their command, oftentimes at significant expense to their own career progression. These leaders would see themselves as more of a conduit between their men and the higher chain of command and would use their position of relative power to enable their subordinates and to go into bat for them when necessary. Furthermore, these leaders would never ask one of their subordinates to do a job that they wouldn't be prepared to do themselves and you would often find them next to their men when there was work to be done, rolling up their sleeves and working as hard as, if not harder than anyone else. When they did have to delegate work out of necessity they would generally make a point of explaining why they couldn't do it themselves, which for the most part was due to a requirement to use their specific skill sets for a higher objective. When there were accolades to be bestowed upon their element they would go to great lengths to ensure that credit was passed down to the lowest level of individual involved, but when there was a shit-storm raining down from above they would take full accountability for their element's failure and umbrella those below them from the spray. Once the barrage from above had been absorbed these leaders would then ensure that those directly responsible for the failure were made aware of it in no uncertain terms, however this would be done in an appropriate, firm and fair manner, and would never constitute throwing the subordinate under the bus to preserve their own reputation. These leaders were truly inspirational, and I was privileged to observe many with these attributes over the years to role model my own leadership style on.

When it came to accolades and praise in the military my philosophy was to be very generous in giving credit where credit was due to those under my command, while not expecting any from my own superiors. Although everyone likes a pat on the head once in a while, I have always been intrinsically motivated and therefore generally found enough satisfaction in simply knowing myself when I had put in my best effort and achieved a set objective. The byproduct of this internal drive to achieve objectives for my own satisfaction would sometimes be recognised by my hierarchy and I would get a pat on the head, or other times it would go completely unrecognised, which was fine by me as well. Overall however I have found that if I simply concentrated on the job in front of me and give it my full attention and best effort the rest would look after itself. I've always disliked those who put on a big song and dance to make sure that the whole world is aware of the job they are doing as to draw praise for any accomplishment achieved. By the same token I disliked those who would happily turn up and put in for the fun and sexy stuff but would cut corners in the more mundane but necessary activities. In the Special Forces medical world, I saw this periodically with medics who only wanted to do the job at the pointy end, getting out and about on combat operations and responding periodically to blown up or shot operators in the heat of the moment. This was certainly a key function of the role and I took it upon myself to ensure that all the medics I had the privilege of commanding were competent in their trade in order to respond in that situation. That was however an assumed skill for any medic who went on operations, and the way that I differentiated an excellent medic from the rest was by the quality of their medical documentation, their ordering of stock and management of stores, their medical planning, and their efforts to further our overall capability through organising training or writing reports. The medics that I worked with over the years would consistently excel in tactical medical situations, and cumulatively saved dozens of lives in the field, but the ones who I rated the highest in their performance appraisals were those who applied as much effort to the mundane administrative functions of the role as they did to the shiny stuff. If you're in a position of leadership I urge you to look past the obvious overt achievements of your subordinates and make a point of recognising those who put in the hard yards in the mundane tasks. In my opinion it is those workers who are the ones most worth keeping.

These principles translate directly into the business world and having been fortunate to be a part of a rapidly growing business myself, I have seen this first hand. By applying the very same principles of concentrating entirely on the task at hand at any given point and completing it to the very best of our abilities, one of the companies I'm involved with, TacMed Australia, has slowly but surely gained a reputation as a leader in its field. Be it product sales or the delivery of training, our ethos is exactly the same; deliver the best possible customer experience with a view to training and equipping the customer with the skills and kit required to potentially save a life under the worst possible conditions. In the early years of the business the Australian market for tactical medical training and equipment was incredibly small and the contracts weren't at all lucrative. It didn't matter, our primary motivation was never the money and our drive to serve our customers was intrinsic and borne out of our knowledge that what we had to offer worked and could actually save lives. Over the years the Australian market for our products and services has grown, creating an environment that has allowed TacMed to expand and take on more and more fulltime employees each year. The leadership style employed within TacMed is the same as described above when talking about the best of the military leaders that I observed during my service. The focus is on the employees' welfare and happiness with less consideration given to the opinion of external entities that might be judging us. As a result, the contracts that were initially measured in the thousands of dollars in the early years of the business are now measured in the hundreds of thousands of dollars. Don't get me wrong, in the grand scheme of businesses TacMed remains a minnow, however the point that I am trying to illustrate is that by keeping your head down, focusing primarily on completing the task at hand to the absolute best of your ability, and remaining more concerned with the opinion of those below you in the chain of command rather than that of those above or around you, the rest will look after itself. What was measured in good performance appraisal results in the military environment now translates into good financial returns in the business world, with the principles remaining identical.

The Only Competition
is You Yesterday

As previously mentioned I grew up with a copy of Max Ehrmann's *Desiderata* on the back of our toilet door and resultantly spent hours of quality thinking time reading and contemplating the content of the poem. One passage from it however took me until my early thirties to fully appreciate; it was the following couple of lines:

If you compare yourself with others, you may become vain and bitter,

For always there will be greater and lesser persons than yourself.

As soon as I discovered that I had some athletic potential in my late teens I became fiercely competitive. My sole focus in life became to get forever fitter and faster, with hindsight not to better myself specifically, but to beat others. I measured my own personal success against my relative performance when compared with other athletes, becoming vain when I beat others and bitter when I didn't. Any improvements in my own personal best times for a given event were largely secondary to the position that time placed me in the race. How others performed was of course completely outside of my control, and my attitude in those days even led me to wish ill of other competitors and derive pleasure from their misfortunes such as flat tires or mechanical failure on the bike leg of a triathlon or tripping over in a running race. It's somewhat embarrassing to admit to now, but at the time that was how I saw the situation; me versus them. Looking back now I can see that this attitude contributed significantly to the slump I fell into after I realised that I was never going to make a career out of professional triathlon. I was completely unable to see anything positive that I may have achieved over the period of my triathlon years and was left with nothing but feelings of personal failure and a degree of resentment towards those who were actually good enough to be living my dream. These negative feelings placed a solid chip on my shoulder that stayed firmly there for another decade or so, and while I consider it an unhealthy source of motivation I do actually believe this requirement to prove myself contributed significantly to my drive to excel in the military. More subconsciously than consciously I suspect that my Special Forces aspirations were a way for me to finally put my triathlon "failures" to bed by being able to beat others in that selection process. That was the attitude that I carried with me throughout my twenties as I trained and postured myself towards the SASR selection course, and it was the attitude I still held when I finally lined up next to the 157 other candidates at the start of selection. The three weeks that followed would change my attitude forever after.

From the very moment that the selection course got underway the attrition rate was incredible. Due to the frenetic pace of the course, coupled with the fact that we were regularly broken into smaller groups for activities, it was initially difficult to gauge the rate at which candidates were withdrawing. The Withdrawal at Own Request (WOR) process was very deliberately done away from the main groups, and once they had signed themselves off the course candidates and their equipment were rapidly removed from the training area in a clandestine fashion as not to be visible to those remaining. On the few initial occasions that I did witness a dejected looking candidate here and there in discussion with Directional Staff, or signing their WOR form, it was always only fleeting glimpses as I was running from one activity to the next, and never under circumstances that allowed protracted consideration of what I was witnessing. The first time I remembered actually realising the attrition rate on the course came about five or six days in, when we returned to a communal sleeping area where we had dumped our kit on folding stretchers a couple of days prior, before disappearing for 48 hours on another activity. Upon return I counted about 80 folded stretchers in one corner of the warehouse-sized room, and those stretchers and piles of kit of the remaining candidates looked widely spaced out in the large area where they had previously been packed in with little room to move in between them. I remember drawing great inspiration from the knowledge that about half the course had quit by that stage and that I was still hanging in there. That was the final time I can recall experiencing pleasure and inspiration from the failure of others. Over the two weeks that followed my attitude began to change completely. Through the selection process breaking me down both physically and psychologically I became more and more aware that I wasn't competing with the candidates around me, the only competition was within myself between my mind driving me onward and my body threatening to quit. Through intense mutual suffering I had started to bond with my fellow candidates and actually began to feel saddened when I returned from an activity to find the pile of empty stretchers growing, or realising that someone I had come to know and respect on the course had withdrawn. Towards the end of week two of the course I remember seeing another candidate filling out his WOR form and pleading with him not to, trying to get him to realise that he was well over half way through the course and if he just hung in there it would be over before he knew it. My efforts were futile, and I subsequently watched him hand in his form, crying as he did so, and get whisked away from the group to be returned to his unit. It left me feeling hollow, whereas a week prior the same experience would have pleased me. For the first time I could truly empathise with that fellow candidate, I understood clearly the investment, struggle and sacrifice he had made to get to that point and I could appreciate the devastation he must have felt by quitting on his dreams. As the course intensified towards its sleep and food deprived finale the bonding process between the remaining group also intensified, and the withdrawal of one of us in the final few days was more like the loss of a family member than a competitor. In the closing days of the course I wanted nothing more than for all the remaining candidates to successfully get to the finish line, so much so that had the opportunity presented to sacrifice my own spot on the course for another candidate I may well have taken it. On the very last activity of the course my body began to fail me. An infection that had started in a blister on my heel had progressed up my right leg and was starting to poison my blood, causing me to stumble and fall repeatedly under the weight of my own pack and rendering me completely unable to assist with the carrying of the extra equipment that our group had been allocated as we raced towards the final pickup point of the course. I would have been completely physically unable to reach the final truck had it not been for the assistance of my "competitors" dragging me along and assisting with my pack. Had they have held the same attitude that I had carried throughout my life pre-selection they would have left me in a heap on the dirt road and completed the course without me, but they didn't. It was a truly humbling and enlightening experience that would forever change my view on competition from that period forth.

When the gruelling three-week period finally drew to a

conclusion I was overwhelmingly happy for my fellow candidates who had reached the finish line alongside me and my ranking within that group, as well as whether or not I would be considered suitable for further service with SASR was largely inconsequential to me at the time. I didn't see my performance as having beaten 130 or so other candidates; I saw it as a victory of my mind over my broken body, and of myself and the other finishers against the course. For the very first time I came to realise what the legendary 17th century Japanese swordsman, philosopher, and ronin Miyamoto Musashi was saying in reference to the spirit of a warrior:

Today is victory over yourself of yesterday

The SASR selection course was a turning point in the way I saw competition. Whether it was due to a sense of self-assuredness from being able to successfully accomplish a challenging goal that I had set myself, or perhaps the laying to rest of demons that had plagued me since the failure to realise my triathlon aspirations, I'm not sure. What I do know is that from that time onward I have no longer felt the requirement to measure my achievements relative to that of others, and I have been able to feel a deep sense of happiness in seeing others achieve their aspirations, rather than the previous feelings of resentment that I may have had under the same circumstances. I still believe in striving for excellence and am highly motivated by competition, but that competition now is measured against my previous personal performances rather than those of other athletes or academics in my fields of interest. In recent years I've come to further realise that the feeling of greatest accomplishment comes through not only bettering yourself of yesterday but through being able to bring others along for the ride via either training with them to improve their personal performance, or through motivating them indirectly to strive toward a goal. Nowadays it inspires me to see someone else exceed my own personal capabilities, not necessarily to catch up to them but simply to move further from my own previous limits.

In finishing up this chapter I'd like to leave the reader with a passage from another piece of brilliant literary work that I feel relates to the topic, and one from which the British SAS have adopted the informal motto *always a little further.* The work I'm referring to is the 1913 poem *The Golden Road to Samarkand* written by James Elroy Flecker, which is set in ancient times and describes a caravan compiled of wealthy merchants carrying all manner of riches accompanied by a group of poor pilgrims as they set out on a journey across Central Asia to the city of Samarkand. In the relevant passage the Master of the Caravan turns to the pilgrims and asks:

But who are ye in rags and rotten shoes, you dirty bearded, blocking up the way?

To which the leader of the Pilgrims replies:

We are the Pilgrims, master, we shall go always a little further: it may be beyond the last blue mountain barred with snow, across that angry or that glimmering sea.

I love this passage for the fact that despite being on foot and surrounded by rich merchants on camels the pilgrims are not bitter. They are mission-focused and will stop at nothing to achieve their goal of reaching Samarkand. Where possible, be the Pilgrim!

Don't Leave Things Unsaid, and Never, Ever Take Yourself Too Seriously

As a parting shot I have two final quick points, the first of which is to try not to leave things unsaid.

One relative constant throughout my medical and military careers has been death. Over the course of my professional life I have witnessed all manner of deaths from perspectives ranging from that of a soldier on the battlefield, a doctor working in both the emergency department setting as well as a palliative care capacity, and to the loss of loved ones and family members of my own. I have experienced good deaths and bad ones. I have seen children robbed from their family members by violent and untimely deaths, and experienced the pain of watching grieving parents, spouses, and children of lost family members taken too soon. On other occasions I have had the intimate privilege of being able to help facilitate dignified and pain-free deaths through well-managed palliative care of terminally ill patients, and experienced the humbling gratitude of the families left behind. If I had to identify a single factor that was key in determining the amount of grief associated with death it would be whether everything that needed to be said had been said. I vividly recall the buckling and enduring grief of a particular young lady after the death in a high-speed motorbike accident of her partner following a heated argument between the two. As I'm sure most could imagine having to move on with life after such trauma would be tremendously difficult.

On a personal note, in the recent past prior to writing this book I lost one of my life-long best mates, my dad. As devastating a loss as that was I didn't shed a single tear throughout the process or since owing to the simple fact that nothing remained unsaid between Dad and me. We were somewhat fortunate in that Dad had fought a gallant battle with cancer over a number of years allowing my family time to mentally prepare for his eventual passing and to ensure that everything that needed to be said had been said. Had we have lost Dad more suddenly I don't believe that much would have differed in that we had the privileged relationship whereby we regularly expressed our gratitude and love for one another. In the end Dad's funeral was a wonderful celebration of his life rather than a grieving of his death, and left all in attendance with an overwhelmingly positive memory of the day.

The reality is that we are all going to die one day and we never really know when the swift hand of fate will take us or one of our loved ones away. I encourage everyone to keep that fact in mind and live accordingly. Remind those close to you how you feel about them regularly, and if there's loved ones out there that you've lost contact with or fallen out with over something relatively trivial in the grand scheme of things, reach out to them and reconnect. It may just be the difference between you being able to smile in remembrance of them rather than cry.

The final point that I'd like to leave the reader with before signing off is to try not to ever fall into the trap of taking yourself too seriously. My favourite story illustrating this point comes from a time when I had recently purchased my vintage Lamborghini, and is set in the heat of a Sydney summer. On the day in question I was on leave from work and had decided I would hit the local army base for a quick workout at the gym. My intention was to simply drive to the gym, work out, then drive home with no planned stops in between. I had dressed accordingly with a singlet, shorter-than-regulation running shorts and a set of at the time fashionable Vibram Five-Finger gym shoes. If you're unfamiliar with this style of footwear take a moment now to Google them so that you can have a full appreciation of the following story!

There I was driving my gleaming red Lambo on a perfect summer's day along a main road in Sydney's eastern beach suburbs on my way to the army base. As I went to turn off into the side street that the base was located on I found myself stopped at a red light and glancing in the rear-view mirror I saw a convertable Jeep full of bikini-clad young ladies approaching behind me. As the Jeep pulled to a halt immediately behind my car I watched as the girls began checking out my car and me, and as I tried to ascertain whether they were appreciating what they saw or were simply judging me as a bloke desperately trying to compensate for inadequacies, the traffic light went green. It was at that exact moment as I went to take off from the light that my fickle Italian mistress of a car decided to die completely. Frantically cranking the key was met with absolutely no response, not even the engine trying to turn over, nothing. The green light turned orange, then red, and still not a hint of a response from my car. The car behind the Jeep began to honk and the horrible realisation began to dawn on me that I was going to have to get out and push my car off the road dressed as I was for the gym. Left with no option, I exited the car to the hysterical laughter and clapping of the girls in the Jeep and began the struggle of pushing my car up onto the curb to let the traffic behind me pass. It was humiliating and fantastic all at once and while everyone in the cars that passed was laughing, no one was laughing harder than me. Everyone wants to see the dickhead in the Lamborghini break down, even me, and the fact that I was clad in such revealing gym attire was just icing on the humiliation cake. Thankfully the issue with my car was a simple ignition fuse failure and I was able to replace the fuse and get to the gym for my session after all.

There have been plenty of other similar incidents both

before and after the one outlined above and I'm proud to say that for the most part I have generally always been able to see the humour in the situation and have a good laugh at myself. Like most things in life, we all have a choice as to how we respond in any given situation and if you don't fall into the trap of taking yourself too seriously you can often have a laugh when things go wrong rather than getting angry.

Conclusion

Well there it is, the key motivational philosophies and lessons learned from my transformation from a chubby, average kid to a Special Forces doctor and beyond. There is no extraordinary genetics, luck, or secret sauce, just plain old dreaming big, goal setting, and relentless pursuit of those goals until they were achieved, or they were clearly no longer appropriate or achievable. There is nothing shiny about my journey, which is great news for all of us. We are all capable of greatness, however we may define that as individuals, with persistence being the key ingredient that will separate us from others who might fall short of their goals. I truly hope that at least one or two points in this book have resonated with you and possibly inspired you to set a goal towards self-improvement. If that is the case, then I'd love to hear from you – DM me on Instagram and let me know. As I've mentioned a number of times we only get one go at this life so don't become comfortable and settle if you're truly convinced that you're destined for something more. Get started today, set an ambitious goal, and go out there and smash it!

About the Author

Dan Pronk had a profoundly average Australian upbringing, the son of an army helicopter pilot father and speech therapist mother, he had one brother and a cat growing up. After attending seven schools and getting expelled from one, he graduated high school with average grades and began the ambitious pursuit of a career in professional triathlon. Five years later when that failed, on a whim he applied for the army and sat the entrance test for medical school, being successful in both and setting him on a trajectory to becoming an army doctor.

A year later an encounter with a group of Special

Forces soldiers led to a lightbulb moment for Dan, he *had* to join Special Forces and be a part of what they do. The only problem was it would be six years before he would be allowed on the Special Forces selection course. Undeterred, Dan set his sights on Special Forces selection and year-in, year-out bettered himself with a view to passing the course. In 2008 Dan successfully completed the Australian Special Air Service Regiment's selection course and went on to become one of Australian Special Operations' most highly deployed and decorated doctors.

After five years with Special Forces Dan discharged to pursue a career in civilian medicine, as well as further study in the form of a Master of Business Administration. Demons from Dan's military time would catch up with him after discharge and following a period of struggle with Post-traumatic Stress, he emerged out the other side a stronger person, experiencing Post-traumatic Growth. Post-army Dan has gone on to an executive role in medical management, as well as co-owning the multimillion dollar company TacMed Australia and founding several other entrepreneurial startups. He stays engaged with tactical medicine through serving as a board member of the Australian Tactical Medical Association and as the medical director of TacMed. He lives in South Australia with his wife and three boys and drives his vintage Lamborghini in the hills whenever he can.

To find out more about this book or
to contact the author, please visit:
www.vividpublishing.com.au/70kg

Printed in June 2023
by Rotomail Italia S.p.A., Vignate (MI) - Italy